Immortelle and Bhandaaraa Poems

Lelawattee Manoo-Rahming

ISBN: 978-988-8228-57-7

Immortelle and Bhandaaraa Poems is Lelawattee Manoo-Rahming's second collection of poetry. It was shortlisted for the inaugural international Proverse Prize.

Inspired by the Hindu philosophy of reincarnation, many of the poems in this new collection are written in memory of loved ones. But, in the same way that the orange and red flowers of the Immortelle tree flame the forests and plains of Trinidad, these poems are brightened with imagery of hope and rebirth. The brilliant flowers of the Immortelle tree also evoke the flames in Hindu cremation ceremonies. Thirteen days after the cremation, Bhandaaraa puja is performed to help the newly-released soul depart this earthly plane. These poems are like the Bhandaaraa prayers that feed the souls of the dead and the living.

Manoo-Rahming's *Immortelle and Bhandaaraa Poems* is filled with scenes from the poet's physical landscape which spans the Caribbean: from The Bahamas, her present home, to Trinidad, the land of her birth. The language of these sensual poems is a syncretism of her East Indian-derived Bhojpuri Hindi and her Trinbagonian creole, peppered with nuances of the Bahamian vernacular. This syncretism is reflected in the themes of the poems. Although many of the poems deal with Indo-Caribbean anthropology, the collection embraces other cultures and religions which are present in the Caribbean, and speaks to the fluidity in philosophy that can exist and flourish in such plural societies.

Immortelle and Bhandaaraa Poems is a celebration of life and a testament to the lives of those who have passed on.

The Glossary and Notes give careful explanations of the many references to specific religions and cultures and the wide-ranging vocabulary, including from local patois.

Immortelle and Bhandaaraa Poems

Lelawattee Manoo-Rahming

Finalist for the inaugural Proverse Prize

Proverse Hong Kong

Immortelle and Bhandaaraa Poems
by Lelawattee Manoo-Rahming
2nd pbk ed. pub. in Hong Kong by Proverse Hong Kong,
July 2016.
Copyright © Proverse Hong Kong, July 2016.
ISBN: 978-988-8228-57-7
Available from https://createspace.com/6366745

Ebook ed., pub. in Hong Kong by Proverse Hong Kong, April 2012.
ISBN: 978-988-19935-3-3

1st pub. in pbk in Hong Kong by Proverse Hong Kong, 9 March 2011.
Copyright © Proverse Hong Kong, 9 March 2011.
ISBN 978-988-19321-3-6

1st ed. pbk distribution (Hong Kong and worldwide):
The Chinese University Press of Hong Kong, The Chinese University
of Hong Kong, Shatin, New Territories, Hong Kong SAR.
E-mail: cup-bus@cuhk.edu.hk   Web site: www.chineseupress.com

Enquiries to: Proverse Hong Kong, P. O. Box 259, Tung Chung Post
Office, Tung Chung, Lantau Island, NT, Hong Kong SAR, China.
E-mail: proverse@netvigator.com
Web: www.proversepublishing.com

The right of Lelawattee Manoo-Rahming to be identified as the author
of this work has been asserted by her in accordance with the Copyright,
Designs and Patents Act 1988.

Page design by Proverse Hong Kong. Cover image 'Immortelle' by and
© Lelawattee Manoo-Rahming. Cover design, Proverse Hong Kong
and Artist Hong Kong Company.

All rights reserved. No part of this publication may be reproduced, stored in a retrieval system, or transmitted, in any form or by any means, electronic, mechanical, photocopying, recording or otherwise, without the prior written permission of the publisher or publisher and author. The book is sold subject to the condition that it shall not, by way of trade or otherwise, be lent, re-sold, hired out or otherwise circulated without the publisher's or author's and publisher's prior written consent in any form of binding or cover other than that in which it is published and without a similar condition including this condition being imposed on the subsequent owner or purchaser. Please contact Proverse Hong Kong in writing, to request any and all permissions (including but not restricted to republishing, inclusion in anthologies, translation, reading, performance and use as set pieces in examinations and festivals).

Permissions and Prior Publication Acknowledgements. Note on Original Artwork

The following poems in *Immortelle and Bhandaaraa Poems* have been previously published as follows:

'email to Kamau Brathwaite on his 70th birthday' and 'Hurucan Floyd' were first published in *The Caribbean Writer,* Volume 14, 2000, University of the Virgin Islands, St. Croix, US Virgin Islands.

'Kaiso Fuh Kitchie' was first published in *Poui: The Cave Hill Literary Annual,* Number 3, December 2001, published by the Department of Language, Linguistics, & Literature, University of the West Indies, Cave Hill Campus, Barbados, W.I.

'Sans Humanite' was first published in the journal, *In Our Own Words: A Generation Defining Itself,* Volume 4, 2002, published by MW Enterprises, Raleigh, North Carolina, USA.

'Deya for Ajee', under the previous title 'And the goddess Bhavani created all things', was first published in *Divali 2002,* Volume 3, No. 2, 2002: the Indo-Caribbean Cultural Council (ICC) Divali souvenir magazine, published by the Indo-Caribbean Cultural Council (ICC), Trinidad and Tobago, W.I., 2002.

'Immortelle' was first published in *The Caribbean Writer,* Volume 17, 2003, published by the University of the Virgin Islands, St. Croix, US Virgin Islands.

'A Pantoun in Pink and White' was first published in *The Hampden-Sydney Poetry Review, Poetry of the Caribbean* special issue, Winter, 2004, published by Hampden-Sydney

Immortelle and Bhandaaraa Poems

College, Hampden-Sydney, Virginia, USA.

'Drummer Boy' and 'Memory Catalogue' were first published in *Poui: The Cave Hill Literary Annual,* Number 6, December 2004, published by the Department of Language, Linguistics, & Literature, University of the West Indies, Cave Hill Campus, Barbados, W.I., 2004.

'Healing After Hurricanes Frances and Ivan' and 'The Poet' were first published in *Poui: The Cave Hill Literary Annual,* Number 7, December 2005, published by the Department of Language, Linguistics, & Literature, University of the West Indies, Cave Hill Campus, Barbados, W.I.

'Child ah de Big Bang Forward Home', 'No People Land', 'Guardian of the Threshold', 'Oleander Sestina' and 'Guanahani' were first published in *Anthurium: A Caribbean Studies Journal* – the online literary journal of the University of Miami, Volume 4, Issue 1, Spring 2006, published by the University of Miami, Coral Gables, Florida, USA.
http://anthurium.miami.edu/volume_4/issue_1/V4I1index.html

'The Colour of Rape' was first published, and 'Drummer Boy' was second time published in *Yinna: The Journal of the Bahamas Association for Cultural Studies,* Volume 2, August 2007, a publication of the Bahamas Association for Cultural Studies (BACUS), published by Guanima Press Ltd., Nassau, NP, Bahamas.

'Life/Death/Life Mothering', 'Parang Serenade in Two Parts', 'Boundary Ball Victory' and 'Bad Hair Night' were first published in the *Journal of Caribbean Literatures,* Volume 5, Number 3, published by Balfour Printing, Little

Rock, Arkansas, USA, 2008.

'Mirror Glimpses' was first published in *ANIDE: Asociación Nicaragüense de Escritoras*, Año 8, Edición No. 20, Enero – Junio 2009, published by Asociación Nicaragüense de Escritoras, Managua, Nicaragua.

'Flight of the Osprey' was first published in *tongues of the ocean* – the online literary journal of Bahamian, Caribbean and related poetry, 2009 October Issue. http://tonguesofthe ocean.org/2009/10/flight-of-the-osprey/

'Deya for Ajee', under the previous title, 'And The Goddess Bhavani Created All Things', was republished in ed. Lynn Sweeting, *The WomanSpeak Journal*, Vol. 5, Nassau, The Bahamas, The WomanSpeak Press, 2010.

'Vaginal Scan' was first published in the anthology, *Caribbean Erotic*, ed. Opal Palmer Adisa and Donna Aza Weir-Soley, Leeds, UK, Peepal Tree Press, 2010.

Epigraphs to selected poems in Lelawattee Manoo-Rahming's *Immortelle and Bhandaaraa Poems* **are acknowledged as follows:**

'Hurucan Floyd': from, Derek Walcott, 'Hurucan', in Derek Walcott, *Collected Poems 1948-1984*, Faber and Faber Limited, London, 1992.

'Guardian of the Threshold': from a statement by Robert Kelly, as quoted in Celia Bland, "Poetry is Doors: An Interview with Robert Kelly", *Poets and Writers*, May/June 2004, Poets and Writers Inc., New York.

'The Poet': from Daniel Ladinsky's translation of a poem by Hafiz (c. 1320-1389), as quoted by Daniel Ladinsky in his Introduction to his translations of Hafiz, *The Subject Tonight Is Love: Sixty Wild and Sweet Poems of Hafiz*, Penguin Compass, New York, 2003.

'The Birthing Season – India In Spring': from Rabindranath Tagore (1861-1941), 'Song of the Blossoming Champak', in his, *The Cycle of Spring*, Rupa and Co., New Delhi, India, 2002.

'email to Kamau Brathwaite on his 70th birthday': from Benjamin Zephaniah, 'As an African', in his poetry collection, *City Psalms*, Bloodaxe, 1992. (Reference kindly sourced by Dr Sandra Paquet.)

Original artwork in print editions

All original artwork as follows: – 'Immortelle', 'Mandala', 'Loofah', 'Full Moon Healing', 'Coatrischie', 'Two Weeks Later', 'Children of Orion', 'Hat with Coconut Rachis', 'Reincarnation' by and © Lelawattee Manoo-Rahming.

Symbols on section pages, representing the different goddesses, original artwork by and © Lelawattee Manoo-Rahming.

Cover image 'Immortelle' by and © Lelawattee Manoo-Rahming.

Author's Acknowledgements

Immortelle and Bhandaaraa Poems would not have been possible without the support and encouragement of many persons. I would like to thank Lorna Goodison for critiquing an early draft of the collection, for having faith in the work and for being my poetry mentor. I would also like to thank Drs. Gillian and Verner Bickley, Founders of Proverse Hong Kong, for creating the Proverse Prize, the Proverse Prize judges for short-listing *Immortelle and Bhandaaraa Poems* for the inaugural prize, and Proverse Hong Kong for publishing the collection. Special thanks go to the Proverse editorial team for their careful and thoughtful work. I am deeply grateful to Dr. Sandra Pouchet Paquet for writing the Preface and for doing so with great sensitivity and scholarship. Dr. Sandra Pouchet Paquet was the Director of the Caribbean Writers Summer Institute at the University of Miami, where I had my first poetry workshop, with Lorna Goodison, and I am grateful for that literary space and the connections it created.

I would also like to thank all of my family, especially my husband, Hammond Rahming and my sisters, Madoorie Primchand and Kamla Patino, for allowing me the space to create and for believing in the work. To all of my artist and writer friends, particularly Dionne Benjamin-Smith, Dr. Christian Campbell, Marion Bethel, Lynn Sweeting, Helen Klonaris and Dr. Jennifer Rahim, I thank you for your encouragement and support. Warmest thanks to all of my readers and lovers of poetry.

Table of Contents

Preface by Sandra Pouchet Paquet	15

The Goddess Bhavani Created All Things

Deya for Ajee	21
Mirror Glimpses	26
Washerwoman	28
Lemoned Leaves	30
My Dear Laxhmie Kumarie	32
Bhandaaraa Puja for Sundar Popo Uncle	33
Child ah de Big Bang Forward Home	35
Immortelle	38
Kaiso fuh Kitchie	40
When Goddesses Grieve	42
Memory Catalogue	44
A Pantoun in Pink and White	45
Life/Death/Life Mothering	48

Goddess Durga, The Unapproachable, Represents The End of All Things

Boundary Ball Victory	51
Flight of the Osprey	53
Colours of Daddy	54
Drummer Boy	55
Canna Lilies and Caterpillars	56
Joe Monks Blues	57
Waiting for Blackface	59
Oleander Sestina	60
The Colour of Rape	62
Sans Humanite	64`

Coatrischie: Tempest-Raising Goddess of The Antilles

No Grouper Days	67
Hurucan Floyd	68
Healing After Hurricanes Frances and Ivan	71
In the Time of Hurricane Jeanne	72
Fish-hooks and masks	73
Clifton Cay	74
An Ode to Peace	75
What if the B-S Axis Revolved Around Maha Lakshmi	77
No People Land	78
Pink Wall Blues	79
Invasive Species on Buck Island, United States Virgin Island	81

Hecate, Queen of the Night: Women Evoked Hecate for Protection and Erected Her Threefold Images at their Doors

Guardian of the Threshold	84
Give Me Your Chaff and Grain	85
Pearl in the Oyster	86
Vaginal Scan	87
My Coontie	88
Bad Hair Night	89
Past Prime Time	91
Ghazal on Ageing	92
Acne on God's Cheek	94

The Goddess, as the Shakti or Energy of Divinity, Surrounds and Animates the Energy of the Male God

Strong Like Mangrove	96
Ocean Goddess on a Journey	98
The Night the Scorpion Ate the Moon	100
The Wild Lover	102
Desert Rose	103
Guanahani	104
Reggae Music	105
The Poet	106
email to Kamau Brathwaite on his 70th birthday	107
The Birthing Season – India in Spring	110
Finding Shakti	112
Divali 2003	114
Parang Serenade in Two Parts	115
The Poet	118
The Preface writer	120
Glossary	121

Table of Illustrations – Original artwork by Lelawattee Manoo-Rahming
Print editions only

Art-work	Related poem	Page
Mandala *Crayon and acrylic on paper, 9in x 12in original size*	Deya for Ajee	20
Loofah *Pen and ink on paper, 18in x 12in original size*	Washerwoman – for Sally	29
Immortelle *Collage of paper and whelk shell on paper, 9in x 12in original size*	Immortelle – In Memory of Ras Shorty	37
Coatrischie *Collage of paper and acrylic paint on paper, 9in x 12in original size*	Life/Death/Life/Mothering	47
Full Moon Healing *Collage of paper on paper, 9in x 12in original size*	Waiting for Blackface	58
Two Weeks Later *Collage of dried flowers and leaves with acrylic paint on paper, 9in x 12in original size*	Past Prime Time	90
Children of Orion *Pen and ink on paper, 24in x 36in original size*	Acne on God's Cheek	93
Hat with Coconut Rachis *Charcoal on paper, 12in x 18in original size*	Ocean Goddess on a Journey	97
Reincarnation *Collage of recycled clothes labels, stamps, paper doilies and cord on paper, 9in x 12in original size*	The Birthing Season – India In Spring	109

Preface

There is a double reward for the reader of this collection of poetry by Lelawattee Manoo-Rahming, in that it includes nine of her art works that correspond by title to specific poems in the volume. The tension generated by the proximity of the visual works and the poems transforms the reading experience of both and generates strong cross-resonance between the two genres. Representation is split and new ambiguities are introduced; the drama of reading is intensified and complicated in new and irresolvable ways. Lelawattee Manoo-Rahming is a poet and mixed media artist of great range and complexity; all of the world and its myriad experiences are her concern.

Lelawattee Manoo-Rahming was born and educated in Trinidad and makes her home in the Bahamas where she is a practicing engineer. Best known as a poet, she is also a prize-winning writer of short fiction and a mixed media artist, who is prominent among a new group of Caribbean women poets who write about the Indo-Caribbean experience.[1] Like Mahadai Das (1954-2003) and Rajandaye Ramkissoon-Chen (1936-2009), Shani Mootoo and Ramabai Espinet, Lelawattee Manoo-Rahming is a poet who writes about the complex experiences of generations of Indo-Caribbean women who first crossed the Kala Pani as immigrants and indentured labourers in the nineteenth century and settled in the Caribbean. These women poets write from the perspective of the modern Caribbean woman who seeks new ways of conceptualizing the contemporary Indo-Caribbean woman's experience in the Caribbean and

---

[1] To provide some historical perspective on how recent their publications are, consider the dates of publication of these first books: Mahadai Das's *Bones* in 1988, Rajandaye Ramkissoon-Chen's *Ancestry* in 1997, Ramabai Espinet's *Nuclear Seasons* in 1991, Shani Mootoo's *The Predicament of Or* in 2000, and Lelawattee Manoo-Rahming's *Curry Flavour* in 2000.

its diaspora, which may be located in North America or Europe, or even in parts of the Caribbean that have no history of East Indian indenture.

Curry Flavour, Lelawattee Manoo-Rahming's first volume of poetry, readily engages the reader with its distinctive Caribbean aesthetics and themes of East Indian arrival, settlement and creolization. Each of the volume's ten sections begins with a Hindu prayer in homage to ancestry, and each deepens to name the grief and joy of resettlement in the Caribbean in the culturally specific terms of the individual, family, and community. The poet's spiritual and material frame of reference is Hindu and Creole, and it is also Bahamian. She celebrates Trinidad's Carnival and Calypso as well as Bahamian Junkanoo. The rhythm of her poetry reflects the multiple dimensions of a plural Caribbean society, but not uncritically so. Many of her poems speak of abandonment, incest, infertility and violence in a language that stages pain intensely and seemingly without deflection. Yet, in other poems, the poet seems equally unabashed in registering a delight in the sensuous, whether dance or song, sacred or bawdy, sexual or culinary erotic. The poet's voice emerges out of a varied selection of events and conditions in which she secretes herself, in poems that range from the reverential 'Ode to My Unknown Great-Great Grand Mother,' to the anguished 'Leaf-of-life Hands,' and the erotic title poem 'Curry Flavour.' The poet astonishes, disturbs and delights with her distinctive blend of different languages, cultures, settings, and mythologies to register an identity valorized by communion with others.

Her second collection, *Immortelle and Bhandaaraa Poems*, strikes a different register. The poet's distinctive voice seems less exuberant and more apprehensive of mortality and the persistence of evil in the world. Echoing the framework of the preceding collection, each of this volume's five sections is named respectively for the Hindu goddesses Bhavani, and Durga, the Taino goddess Coatrischie, the Greek goddess Hecate, and the Hindu Goddess Shakti. The poet frames her creative efforts in solidarity with sacred and iconographic emblems of womanhood that are familiar and remote, archival and archaeological. Her voice is constructed culturally and reactively in a series of poems written in memory of family, friends and cultural icons whom she identifies as shaping influences in her life and work. This is the work of mourning: writing about the crisis engendered in the poet by the loss she reads into the individuals memorialized.

In the title poems 'Immortelle' and 'Bhandaaraa Puja for Sundar Popo Uncle,' Ras Shorty and Sundar Popo are each revered for their cultural openness and creative communion with other cultures: Ras Shorty for blending the music of India and Africa in Soca, and Sundar Popo for "the sangeet, your courageous goal / Mixing Bhojpuri Hindi and Creole." They, among others like Andre Tanker, Lord Kitchener, Joe Monks and Chris Moxey, valorize a way of being-in-the-world that the poet embraces. She confronts mortality in the death of cultural icons whom she reveres for their artistic talents and cultural values. The poet names herself through the iconographic and the tragic, as well as the reverential and the sacred. In 'When Goddesses Grieve,' the brutal murder of Angela Cropper's family prompts a search for "the sacred / Message" that will bring some comfort to the grief stricken. The absent dead are made present in the sensibility of the poet through the act of naming and a selective identification with the deceased. The poem 'Memory Catalogue' seems to sum up the fragile process of figuration in which the past is remembered and renewed in the present. In 'Oleander Sestina' there is the troubling perception of mortality in the limitations of an individual life, and rage for the victims in 'The Colour of Rape' and 'Sans Humanite.' But there is also a riotous energy, wit and humor in poems like 'Ocean

Goddess on a Journey,' 'The Night the Scorpion Ate the Moon' and 'The Birthing Season – India in Spring' that engage and delight the reader with the keen intelligence and ingenuity of its satirical voice.

These collected works range in both content and tone from the sacred to the profane, from grief to joy, and the journey both in its language and vision is impressive and courageous. Manoo-Rahming guides the reader through national, regional, and familial history while simultaneously revealing, mourning and celebrating her diverse cultural inheritance.

Sandra Pouchet Paquet, Ph.D.
Professor Emerita of English, University of Miami

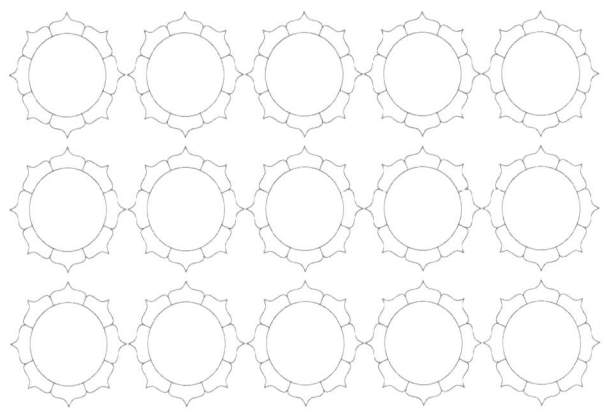

THE GODDESS BHAVANI

CREATED ALL THINGS

'**Mandala' by Lelawattee Manoo-Rahming**

Immortelle and Bhandaaraa Poems

Deya For Ajee
For Lackpatia Deosaran (c. 1909-1999).

I

You were born in the month of Baisakh
When the Sun danced
An orange waltz with Aldebaran
Across the Bull's neck
And the Full Moon kissed
Blue-white Spica on the Virgin's hip.
The Tongue of the Ocean
Licked the caul from your eyes

Moray eels twisted your umbilical cord
Wrapped it tight
And bit the blood-filled tube
Setting you free from Mount Mandara.
Manta rays caught you on their wings
Flew to shallow waters
Tossed you into the air so you landed
On a leatherback turtle

Who lumbered ashore with you on her back
And babies in her egg-filled belly.
Bhavani, Grandmother Goddess, cupped
You in her arms strong like trunks
Of Seaside Coral Bean trees, blew
Into your mouth
Fed you seven-year apple
And promised immortality.

II
But the Great Mother never
Gave you soapberries
To wash away the stain
On your breasts indelible
As red abeer mixed with banana
Sap sprayed wantonly on spring
White saris in Phagwa dances.
Sita, the Ramayan's embodiment

Of purity did not tell you
About Rawan's charm.
How she chose stability over passion.
So when you left your husband
To be with my Ajaa none tested you
By making you walk through fire.
Everyone just called you slut.
You needed another Hanuman

Another Monkey God to cross
Not the sea to Lanka
But the Kala Pani to Chinitat.
To save you from demons
Only you could see floating
Down from Paradise Hill
To Dinsley Plain. Jumbies
Crowding your tapia house

Stealing your amchar massala.
Ajaa wore white suits
White pointed shoes
While pulling Porterweed
In the Raj Garden.
Burning green wild sage
To smoke out mosquitoes,
Clearing away the forested

Humid nursery bed
Of ripe chataigne seeds,
Breeding mongoose to feast
On Mapepire snakes.
The Raj wanted Eden
El Dorado but no Hades.
Ajaa promised to make you
Queen. He never told you

He meant Rum Ranee.
That he would intoxicate you
Not with moonlight passion
But with moonshine dharu.
That he would die under your
White chador surrounded
By white-dirt walls not the stone
Fortification of a palace.

III

Mother Saraswati played celestial music
On the veena as you worshiped
Her begging the Goddess of Learning
For enlightenment. She kept you
Ignorant that one day you would enjoy
Swallowing your children whole,
Sucking their children and spitting
Them out like pomegranate seeds.

Immortelle and Bhandaaraa Poems

Maha Lakshmi, whom you prayed
To for prosperity every Divali
Promised jewels in return for milk
And ghee oblations but all you got
Were wormy pigeon peas
That you sold each Saturday morning
Before playing your whe-whe mark
With market-woman pennies.

You hoped Goddess Durga would spring
From your mouth in the same way she sprang
From the gods' mouths as flames.
You wanted to mount a lion and ride forward
To your enemies like Durga advancing
On the demon Mahisa in buffalo disguise
Whom she slaughtered but the only things
That sprang from your mouth were curses

And cruel words that grew a barbed-wire
Barrier between you and the world.
"Eye fete up wid aallyu"
And we laughed behind your back
"Which fete yuh carry we to Ajee?
Ah carnaval fete? Ah blockorama?"
We had already learnt you were fed up
With us even while we were foetuses.

IV

You died in the arms of your daughter
And daughter-in-law attended
By handmaidens – the white moon sailing
With the Scorpion Mother in broad daylight.
No one knew your age
Only that you outlived your husband
Two sons and three grandsons
And that your hair was pale-as-time yellow.

As my Tanty poured cool water over you
For your morning bath
Your breath escaped and flowed water-like
Into the waiting earth ready with fire
To accept your weathered body
Bleached and pitted as a discarded
Conch shell back into Mount Mandara
Absorbed by Grandmother Goddess Bhavani.

From whom all things are born
And to Whom all things return.
Ajee, I write this poem as I light a deya
To your memory. May Lakshmi Mata
Give me wisdom to find your grit in me.
To see in you my Goddess Durga
Helping me to battle the demons of this life.

Mirror Glimpses
For my mother Dolly Manoo (1937-2001)
and my sister Sally Rajkumarie Deosaran (1959-2000).

Mama your face followed
me to this place. It hopped
a ride in my genes
like the scorpion
that smuggled itself
from Long Island to Nassau
in my bag of cookies.
I took it as a sign:
Sally will die.

Mama your face lives with me
in my house, shadows
my movements
never face to face
only glimpses in the mirror.
Fold of the skin
from nose to chin
In Sally's sunken cheeks.

Mama your face hides from me.
It stares at me behind
my back. I glance sideways
at the curl of your lips
strung between darkened
downturned corners of your mouth,
that doesn't smile any more.
Sally's laughter echoes.

Immortelle and Bhandaaraa Poems

Mama your face consumes me:
which of your grandmothers'
halogen eyes did you steal
to make your skin glow
like a Chinese lantern;
soft fire, burnt sienna?
Her face worm-rotted Mama,
Sally is gone.

Washerwoman
For Sally Rajkumarie Deosaran (1959-2000).

Squish squish squish
You wash
Like a washerwoman at de riverside
Never Dirty, Caura, Matura,
But you couldn't leave your burdens
Let them spin away
Like bois cano leaves sailing
On invisible currents

Squish squish squish
You squeeze
Shame and muck from yards and yards
Of sari cloth soiled by groping hands
You jook them clean and wrap up
Your one baby your preemie girlchild
To keep she warm when de baby father
Put allyuh out like dogs one midnight

Squish squish squish
You squash
Your dreams making suds and foam
You blow soap bubbles watch
The soaring rainbow coloured balls
Bright as Surya's sunlight
You whisper, "Ah doh want she
Tuh have a hard life like me"

Squish squish squish
Your hands no longer hurt
Squish squish squish
No more blood to cleanse
Just your spirit escaping squooshhhhh
Like air in the squish squish squish
Sounds your teenage daughter knows
When she steps in her tennis shoes

'Loofah' by Lelawattee Manoo-Rahming

Immortelle and Bhandaaraa Poems

Lemoned Leaves
For Dolly Manoo (1937-2001).

I was missing you even
While you were still alive

I loved you Mama
Searched for you ever since

You left on one of my
Ninth-year nights

Now in my forty-first year
On one of the blazing hot August days

Water flows from your lastson's hands
Juice flows from your firstson's hands

Blood flowed
Sugar sweet to your second baby girl

And on to her daughter
Your last grandbeti

Sour blood flows
Barren from me your middle child

Stopping up that branch
Of your blood line

Blue-voile-winged
Battimamselles fly

Immortelle and Bhandaaraa Poems

Butterflies like lemoned leaves fly
Sailing through razor grass blades

Swaying in a northeast trade wind
That Maha Devi send

Swooswooswoos from Nirvana
To find you for me

Baljugnees blink onnn / off …
Onnn / off … onnn / off in the peas tree

Lighting it up like Christmas tree
Candle

Flies showing me, guiding you

How to fly away
How to whirl free

On blue-grey cremation smoke
How to glide on Maha Devi's breath

Like your ashes floating
Down the Caroni

Coming to roost in mangrove
Like flocks and flocks of Scarlet Ibis

Going home
Going home

My Dear Laxhmie Kumarie
*For Laxhmie Kumarie Vainmati Kallicharan (1951-2002),
Guyanese writer and cultural activist who perished in fire
in January 2002.*

An ancestral call, a ghazal
Mournful malhar rainy season
In celebration of Kali
The Black Mother Shakti spirit

Did your ghungrus sing a tumhri
To ease the tanhai in your life
To call upon Miramen mai
When the shadows overcame you

In your yajna your sacrifice
of life to Yamraj, God of Death
Through fire from Sun God Suruj
Your cremation without witness

With no puja no katha hymns
No ghee, no pitch pine scented smoke
Just you and your ghungrus singing
A jhalla climactic tempo

To your vibuthi outstanding
Performance in this Kal Yug age
May your ghungrus sing a prelude
To Nada Brahma immortal sound

Bhandaaraa Puja for Sundar Popo Uncle
In memory of Sundar Popo b. Sunilal Popo Bahora (1943-2000).

My dear departed Uncle this me now
Burning incense chanting puja bhajans
Conjuring your image like magician
Making bhakti to your memory vow

To keep the chutney spirit fully fed
Rikki Jai win the Chutney Soca Crown
With a dub/chutney remake of your song
Scorpion sting meh, ah feeling ah go dead

Drupatie singing a filmi gita
Join up with Machel the Calypsonian
Making waves with a soca/dub/Indian
Tune to make me thank Lakshmi Mata

For your good fortune and trailblazer fame
A pioneer songwriter singerman
Building road from Deep South for Sonny Mann
Young Drupatie and Rikki Jai who came

Behind like Nani in your composition
Nana challo age age
Nani going behind
Nana drinking white rum
And Nani drinking wine

Sundar Popo mamoo I have to say
Thanks for the sangeet, your courageous goal
Mixing Bhojpuri Hindi and creole
Climbing the stage all alone for no pay

Immortelle and Bhandaaraa Poems

Sundar Popo this is your bhandaaraa
This camphor and pitch pine smoke aartee
This chant to Bhagwan for your delivery
Into a chutney/soca utopia

Hari Krishna, Hari Krishna,
Hari Rama, Rama, Rama,
Krishna, Krishna, Hari, Hari,
Rama, Rama, Hari, Hari.

Child Ah De Big Bang Forward Home
For Andre Tanker (1941-2003).

De Friday before carnival
What ah time tuh fly away
Tuh look fuh another home
Andre, Boy, ah nevah get ah chance
Tuh tell yuh dat meh young brother
Did well like yuh song *Forward Home*
Ah wonder if he was singing
Dem words as he was floating face
Down in de foam @ Blanchisseuse

Ah went away
Ah leave an ah forward home
Ah forward to stay
Ah must see meh way

De Friday before carnival
Did de lady wid de head-wrap
Ring de bell up and down de street
Sing *sayamanda, sayamanda*
sayamanda an ring she bell
From pole to pole Toco to Sando
From lighthouse blues to crestle greens
Salt-fish buljol roast bake lavway
Ah soca chokha tuh carry
Yuh soul from Port-of-Spain
To Mesopotamia
Like a Wild Indian chant

De Friday before carnival
All de children getting ready
Fuh de Big Bang Jouvert Jab Jab
Ent see naked Ymoja chip
An ramachez tuh ah rapso
Wave song @ Manzanilla beach
How she call yuh in wind music
Like 3canal call yuh tuh practice
De Ben Lion kaiso riddum
How Ymoja rub yuh head wid oil
Whisper yuh is de fire earth
Water free now yuh'll see yuh way

Immortelle and Bhandaaraa Poems

'Immortelle' by Lelaattee Manoo-Rahming

Immortelle and Bhandaaraa Poems

Immortelle

In memory of Ras Shorty b. Garfield Blackman (1941-2000).

When you sang *Indrani*
Your euphony woke me
From a sleep beneath
The Pitch Lake.

I emerged black
Hungry for your SOCAH
Music, your blending
Of India and Africa

Lord Shorty I wanted to be
Your *Indrani – your East Indian Chick*
To follow you into Piparo Forest
Like Sita accompanying Rama
Into his forested banishment

Ras Shorty I Rastafari
I wanted to forsake my puja flowers
Let orange Immortelle flowers substitute
For my perfumed yellow Champa

Magenta Crepe Coq replace
My white rose-petaled Chamelli
Wrap myself in a bleached cotton sari

Sling a dholak around my neck
Step into my wood & rubber sapat
And drum/follow the resonance
Of your chant across the Arena Dam

Om Shanti Om Shanti Shanti Om
Shanti Shanti Om

Immortelle and Bhandaaraa Poems

I wanted to stand before you
And dress my naked body
In ropes and ropes
Of your greying dreadlocks

Pretend you were shrouding
Me from Rawan's lustful gaze
But I was no celibate Sita
You were no Rama

No King of Kosala
Only a Calypso King
Garfield Blackman
Father of a clan

A Rastafari in Piparo
A musical Moses
With a honeyed voice

And a conscious rhythm
A true Trini in exile
In the spirit world

Immortelle and Bhandaaraa Poems

Kaiso Fuh Kitchie
In memory of Lord Kitchener b. Aldwyn Roberts (1922-2000).

De Grandmaster dead!
A month before de 2000 Carnaval
Kitchie just ups and join de Toco Band[2]
Buzzing he way
Like a Bees Melody
Making haste to the greatest
Panorama Finals

He eh waiting for no Rainorama
Or blockorama
Not even Audrey
Wit she sugar bum bum
could stop he. De Flag Woman
wave and wave but the Road
March King eh checking

He dingolay a lil bit
By the Northstand
Then fly like a soucouyant
To Macaripe. Miss Tourist
Was looking good in she g-string
But Lord Kitchener
Eh have no time for dat

---

[2] "Toco Band", "Bees Melody", "Rainorama", "Audrey", "The Flag Woman", "Miss Tourist", "Pan in A-minor", "One to Hang" are some of Lord Kitchener's calypsos.

He busy with he kaiso lyrics
And making sure Boogsie tune
Dat Pan in A-minor just right
Otherwise is One to Hang
Because this is one Road March
Kitchie cyar lose
Not even SuperBlue wit he Ethel[3]

Could beat the Grandmaster this time.
Sparrow could keep he title
Calypso King of the World
But Kitchener will get his Trinity Cross
Because he winning the final
Road March in de biggest Carnaval
Dat never stop in Nirvana

---

[3] One of SuperBlue's calypsos. SuperBlue was a protégé of Lord Kitchener.

Immortelle and Bhandaaraa Poems

When Goddesses Grieve
For Angela Cropper in memory of John Cropper (c. 1941-2000), Maggie Lee (c. 1917-2000) and Lynette Lithgow (c. 1949-2000).

Achall on hill grieving
Her beloved brother;
Mournful cry of Aedon
Heartbroken nightingale;
Airmed's magical herbs
That sprang from Miach's grave;
Meleager's fratricide
Desolate Mother Althaea;

Banshee's keening sorrow;
Carman's destructive sons
Darkness, evil, violence:
Dub, Dother, Dian;
Weeping Goddess Demeter
Searching for her daughter;
Shaven, tattered Isis
Bringing her lover back to life.

I hunger for the rites,
The herbs, the magic spells
To divine the sacred
Message, allegory,
Metaphoric legend
Of springtime renewal
Or autumnal beauty
Reincarnation in this world.

But I am no Goddess
I cannot make magic:
Hazel tree (Coll Buana)
Nor herbs grow from their graves.
I know not embalming
Secrets of Isis wise.
I can only beg Carman
Cull her sons Dub, Dother, Dian.

Say it ain't so, Buan
Not accident, senseless.
Tell me there was meaning
To their slashed throats.
Show me the mystery myth,
Teach me to understand,
Give me psychic power
To read answers in these visions.

Memory Catalogue

Nearly thirty yrs
And everyday
We forget a little more
A name like Pinky
A fruit like caimate or balata
A gummyness gluing up your lips
A malju ward-off charm
Pin up on the baby vest
A seer man or woman
Predicting the jumbie bird cry
A batfilled sky @ dusk
The smell of mango @ midnight
A pretty-faced sixteen-yr-old
With the "*seim* problem"[4] smiling
Same as always picking beans
Alive one day dead the next
A white-dressed corpse
Suicide was not
A known word
Whispers spoke
Of an angry mother dashing
A pretty-faced head
Against
A wall

---

[4] *Seim:* Hindu name for hyacinth beans pronounced "same".

A Pantoun in Pink and White

Pink and white shells broken
Crushed skeletons of gaulin crabs
Pink and white sand fringing
A frothy sea whipped by winds

Crushed skeletons of gaulin crabs
Pink and white visions
A frothy sea whipped by winds
Whistling screaming screeching

Pink and white visions
Seagulls searching for snappers
Whistling screaming screeching
Ethereal in the night

Seagulls searching for snappers
In a blue and white sea
Ethereal in the night
Children's crying voices

In a blue and white sea
Hemmed in by green green seagrapes
Children's crying voices
A pink and white polka dot memory

Hemmed in by green green seagrapes
Leaves hidden by dirty brown
A pink and white polka dot memory
A little girl's Christmas dress

Leaves hidden by dirty brown
Spent and stringy powder puff orbs
A little girl's Christmas dress
Slathered with dried ochre mud

Spent and stringy powder puff orbs
Yesterday's pink and white flowers
Slathered with dried ochre mud
Streaks on her blueblack legs

Yesterday's pink and white flowers
Pink and white sand fringing
Streaks on limp blueblack legs
Pink and white shells broken

Christmas 2002, Duho Inn, Long Island, Bahamas.

'Coatrischie' by Lelwattee Manoo-Rahming

Life/Death/Life Mothering

Royal Poinciana flames red
Bloodlike agony of birth/death
This curious May month season
Coatrischie's mild moaning wind
Soft whimpering from the Goddess
Mingling with cleansing rain Ganga
Mai flowing to earth to attend
Goddess Saraswati scooping

Up a slipped out dangling foetus
In the folds of her sari white
Returning to the celestial
Abode on Mount Kailash perfect
Leaving behind placenta red
Bloody membranous afterbirth
Mounting cycles of muscle spasms
No valium could quiet down

Only anaesthetized death sleep
Baralgin-induced painless hope
Could eject contraction memories
Replace them with holes empty black
Spaces in the brain to be filled
With tears hopeless full of terror
Desolate for the baby lost
Longing for the Goddess embrace

Immortelle and Bhandaaraa Poems

Community of Devi power
Mothers sisters tanties betis
To clasp the wailing prenatal
Mother-not-to-be limp and frail
Lift unto the bed red-petaled
Scented with sandalwood incense
To pray to Saraswati Mai
For a new child a renewed hope

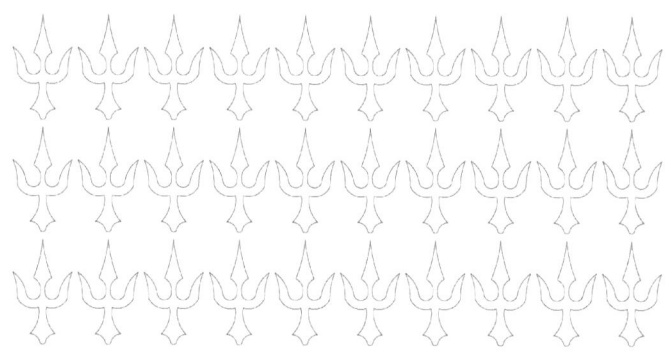

GODDESS DURGA

THE UNAPPROACHABLE

REPRESENTS THE END OF ALL THINGS

Immortelle and Bhandaaraa Poems

Boundary Ball Victory
In memory of Charles Rahming (1935-2005).

All I could vision was cricket
Although your game was basketball.
"The LA Lakers will give
The Detroit Pistons an upset win,"
You predicted in hospital
Bed battling an upset stomach,

Swollen prostate, sluggish bowels.
Were you wishing for an upset
Victory, slam dunk your miscreant
Cells, steal their star shooter thunder?
What about making a century
Chemo after chemo treatment?

But even superstar Lara
Often gets out for duck egg.
First man at the crease and Captain.
Doesn't stop the Windies batting
Running and bowling underdogs
Trying to beat the victors,

Who send them home with lbw's
To armchair critics, bedridden
Former cricketers all who can
Spout what went wrong and why but none
Who now face the enemy side.
Navigating googlies, fielding

Immortelle and Bhandaaraa Poems

After tea on drenched green hoping
That just this day the elements
Will conspire a Windies win.
Bodies not spin-balling themselves.
A boundary ball for six victory
In this cricket match at Life's Oval

Ever since the day I lost
My eighteen-week-old foetus
Your would've-been-eighteenth grandchild
The day I found out about your hurt
Your body riddled with cancer
I wanted to write you this poem

Flight of the Osprey
In memory of Charles Rahming (1935-2005).

The week before
My father-in-law grew
Cold hard as a statue then sprouted
White baptismal wings and flew

I saw an osprey
Soaring above the sea
Where my father-in-law fished
As a little boy

Heard it calling
To spirits caught in the currents
Between earth and sky
Guiding them home

Saw it fishing
For souls lost in the waves
Unable to leave this world
Giving them freedom of flight

And knew
That my father-in-law
Would fly
With the osprey

Colours of Daddy
In memory of Charles Rahming (1935-2005).

Red like tomatoes
Food he grew and fed us
Yellow roses and purple ruellia
He gave us everyday

The Garden in Lebanon
Pomegranates pink ripe
Seeds Holy Word lessons
For this world and the next

Blushed cherry his beaming face
Exploding in laughter
Sea blues his vibrant eyes
Loving us without words

Brown freckled arms
Encircling us with warmth
Golden haired angel
Now guiding us

Immortelle and Bhandaaraa Poems

Drummer Boy
For Chris Moxey (1959-2003).

When you drummed that Junkanoo morn
Ecstatic beat on Boxing Day
Did you fall into a percussive
Trance, did you travel to the crossroads?
Where you met Legba, did he guide
You to the Centre of the World
And show you the Cosmic Tree
Lignum Vitae Tree of Life
Spanning the three worlds?

Did your goatskin drum give you power
Of flight between sky, earth, underworld?
Did you become as swift-footed
As a Long Island goat climbing
The Tree of Life on branches thin
And limber, ever higher
Till you reached the Seventh Heaven
and in your ecstasy forgot
To descend the ladder

From sky to earth back to Bay Street
For the first lap of the parade?
To re-enter your flesh and bones
Complete the Junkanoo Dance
To rush with Saxons one last time?
Did you Drummer Boy become
Shaman and drumbeat a one-way
Passage to Guinea on that cold
Cold, night morning?

Canna Lilies and Caterpillars
For Archdeacon William Thompson (1933-2000).

Canna Lilies grow leaves
Broad to shelter caterpillars
Length and width
Of a man's trigger finger

He covered us with his cloth

Spear-shaped young shoots
Riddled with holes
Same diameter
As the green-juiced borers

The angels sewed shut his bullet-holed artery

Surviving springtime attacks
Lilies blossom scarlet chalices
Eyefeast/nectarfest
For butterflies and moths

He lives, feeds us more bread

Immortelle and Bhandaaraa Poems

Joe Monks Blues
For Joe Monks b. Joseph Weaver (1901-1994).

Joe Monks the boogeyman,
Joseph Weaver the bootlegger,
Joe Monks the USA Boy,
House/picture painter's son.

Joe Monks got sent to jail,
one hundred and nineteen times, he said.

Joe Monks the torpedoed sailor's boy,
Joseph Weaver the jailbird,
Joe Monks the Christmas Baby 1901,
ankle-locked with ball and chain.

Joe Monks got sent to jail,
one hundred and nineteen times, he said.

Joseph Weaver the wicked man,
caused good folks to lock their homes.
When the constable came around,
Joe Monks marked the wall.

Joe Monks got sent to jail,
one hundred and nineteen times, he said.

Long Wharf was Joe's haunt,
sculpting a head with a hatchet and a rock,
fixing skates and making kites,
all the kids called Joseph: friend

Joe Monks got sent to jail,
one hundred and nineteen times, he said.

Immortelle and Bhandaaraa Poems

Joe Monks would rather paint than eat,
getting paper out the garbage
to put pictures on: blue pictures,
yellow pictures, red pictures all

Joe Monks got sent to jail,
one hundred and nineteen times, he said.

Surreal paintings, angry fireworks
from the gravestone builder mason,
Joseph Weaver, 'the crazy man'
Died, 1994, in Sandilands

Joe Monks flew from his jail,
one hundred and nineteen times, plus one.

'Full Moon Healing' by Lelawattee Manoo-Rahming

Waiting for Blackface

Waiting for a heartease
From the silenced mewling
The no more knowledged greeting
No more healing caressing
Mind reading spirit seeing
Loving without favour

Waiting for a respite
From the revolving screams
Piercing the deep dream night
Like canine teeth stabbing
Mauling a little body
Soft belly limber spine

Waiting for a seance
To guide her numinosity
On her shamanic flight path
To channel her wild nature
Safely back to our circle
Protected by deya lights

Waiting for her grave ringed
By guavas to tremble heave
For her cleansed and whole body
To rise on all fours shake off
The loose earth a reversed Sita
Mewling herself alive

Oleander Sestina

Lots of ducks but no breadcrumbs
around the pond lined with oleander,
where we hunched against the drizzle,
past the strolling couple under the red
umbrella that had no seashore
use except maybe to fence in

or hide the copulating pair fenced-in
by inhibitions common as breadcrumbs,
unlike crabs mating on the seashore,
for whom death comes easily, like oleander
poisoning. Bees know to avoid these red
flowers left to fall like a drizzle

on the green salad earth, drizzled
with honey-lime dressing. Fencing,
chain-linked and metallic red,
environmental: rats can feed on breadcrumbs
poisoned with milk of oleander,
their bodies like flotsam on the seashore.

Beached whales and dolphins on the seashore
do not awake in a salty drizzle.
Mystery deaths might as well be oleander
poison from pink-flowered-green-leaved fencing,
hiding bodies scattered like breadcrumbs,
washed out to sea by a frothy red

tide exposing Bleeding Tooth red-
stained eye candy on the seashore.
Polyped seaweed like scattered breadcrumbs
on sand, pock-marked by a drizzle,
remnants of an ocean shower that fenced-in
blue-green lizards in an oleander

prison, like in the movie "White Oleander".
The cell is liberating like the colour red,
a boldness that rejuvenates fenced-in
creativity, fresh like a seashore
breeze foreshadowing a cleansing drizzle,
splattering a canvas with painted breadcrumbs.

Life feeds us breadcrumbs, poisonous oleander
sprays in a drizzle of dangerous red
and a seashore imprisoned by fencing.

The Colour of Rape

What shade of ruby rage
Does a Junkanoo artist paste
On a penis ripping open a vagina?

Does sculpted Brazzalita wood
Bleed carmine
An anus ruptured?

Can we white-out humiliation
Like the waxed-out pattern
In an Androsia batik wrap?

Can a charcoal pencil
Draw grey obscure shape
Of battered self-esteem?

Can sea-green latex
housepaint sheath the dagger
Of rising nausea?

Will an overcoat of gesso
Erase the corrosive
Pigment of desecration?

Is an oil-brushed canvas
Gauze enough to bandage
The victim's sliced-up mettle?

Can we wash the broken
Bodies in watercolour yellow
Hot glue the pieces?

Iron weld them in an orange flux
Let them fuse in a bonfired earth kiln
Heal them whole with pastel-green words?

Sans Humanite

Maybe we can
Burn the rapist
Santimanitay!
Shade our daughters
Reclaim our humanity.

Maybe if we twisted our lips exposed
iron-hot-red sandalwood heart-shaped seeds
nestled in-between brown curly split pods

Maybe we can
Obeah the pusher
Santimanitay!
Grow our sons
Reclaim our humanity.

Maybe if we bared our dilly breasts
sepia sugar juiced grainy fleshed
Amazon-like mothering strong-minded

Maybe we can
Choke the gunman
Santimanitay!
Feed our sisters
Reclaim our humanity.

Maybe if we slowly unfurled our hearts
like sweet-smelling moonlight glory flowers
yellow-lined white blankets to wrap up all

Maybe we can
Smother the murderer
Santimanitay!
Teach our brothers
Reclaim our humanity.

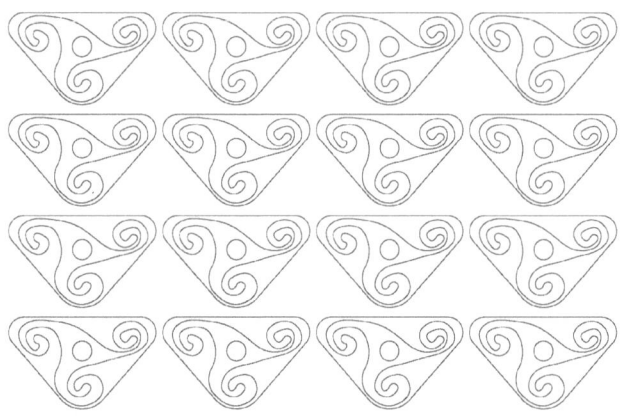

COATRISCHIE

TEMPEST-RAISING GODDESS

OF THE ANTILLES

No Grouper Days

Green-jerry-curled
Mango tree heads bubbled
In the Huracan Floyd stew
Made aqueous, gelatinous
Grey-white with manioc flour

Utility poles and utensiled palms
Toppled top-heavy
Pulling down night-sky tent
Veiling the dawn in black chadors
And Banyan tree branches

Were they fluorescent chimerical days?
Or just sweat-filled cavernous nights?
They were sea-soaked hours without time
But they were no Grouper Days

They were sun-passages
Of dark dreams reality
Salman Rushdie's *Satanic Verses*

They could have been
MuchworsethankGodforLife

Whirling Dervish Days

Hurucan Floyd

...Hurucan.
You Scream like a man whose wife is dead,
like a god who has lost his race,
...A freighter is parked
On the coastal road to the airport,
and the birds won't be back
For some time...
 — Derek Walcott, 'Hurucan'

These days Hurucan
is a shape-shifter:
when she dress up in tailcoat,
we call she names like Floyd;
when she wear cancan and petticoat,
and looking like ooman,
we name she Irene and Lily.

Hurucan come de other day
driving a freighter
like she jetskiing
and park it up right on de coast
road just like the freighter
Derek Walcott see on the airport
road all dem years ago.

Hurucan come to clout up
this yellow-rose-bush in my yard
that so harden it refuse to bloom.
Like it withholding its hellenic beauty
to spite me doh mind I feed
it gobar upon gobar and squeeze
the milk out meh breast so it could drink.

Immortelle and Bhandaaraa Poems

Hurucan just like any other harried
mother and once she start giving licks,
she don't care who right
and who wrong, everybody get
knock down: the tall, tall almond trees;
the skinny casaurina; the banyan
tree wide like a village.

Once Hurucan start lashing,
she vexness just flow like a river.
She twist and twirl,
swirl and roll.
She grumble and throw her arm
this way – a house mashup.
She swish the sea with her swinging
petticoat – a settlement flood out,
a road washway.
Hurucan share licks
for twenty-four hours.
Then she leave.

One week later,
the hardhead yellow-rose-bush
put out buds up and down
its three long, climbing arms.
The banyan tree sprout
green, green like spring.
The house will build back
soon.

Meanwhile everybody looking
but not one could find
the photos Hurucan wrap up
in she kerchief
and stick in she bosom.
All they could see is memories
like wet newspaper
crumbled into muck,
and chimmies feeding
on purple seagrapes.

Healing after Hurricanes Frances and Ivan

Perfumed sage bath for measled skin
Sea stone pumice for calloused heel
Aloes poultice for blisters/burns
Carailli brew for fevered flu
Five Fingers tea for backaches/sprains
Zaboca leaf juice for stillness
Tamarind balls for stopped up bowels
Goat Pepper boil for cleansing blood
Lime and ginger cocktail extract
To refresh our battered dreams
To mend/build our lands and hearths
To make us bloom out of season
Like poinciana blossoming
In September after greening

In the Time of Hurricane Jeanne

Wind sounds like a stormy ocean
When days are rainy dark
Nights are even darker
Like a womb a shielding

Outside world put on hold
Deadlines schedules urgent memos
In liquid suspension
Tornadic winds fuel imagery

Spawning poems surging stories
From darkness welling up
Funneled explosion of energy
Circling the eye not glaucomaed

Not myopic but seeing clearly
Second sight nature's cleansing
Of land and sea cluttered artistry

Fish-Hooks and Masks

Fish-hooks hang
orderly like bars forming a cage.
"Fish-hooks have barbs,"
says the poet as he rubs his finger-tips.
"I don't like them."

Foetuses form rows Egyptian-art like,
rowing across the Middle Passage.
Fishes get snitched
like dead Haitian babies
in the Crooked Island Passage.

Twisted, the better to hook,
nickel alloy thorns do not rust.
They lie preserved in seawater,
silver bone-white-like
salted bones of the Mass Transported.

Fish-hook prickers slide easily
into soft flesh like shark teeth.
Red the colour of blood spurts
when hooks are removed.
Human flesh becomes shark food.

Above the water, safe in wooden boats,
painted-face masks
black women lipsticked silhouettes
crowned with hibiscus blooms
form Junkanoo banner sails.

Shadow Masks hide Mother Agwe's loa
though She still blows on Bahamian sails
protecting Her children
who call Her Mary, Star of the Sea,
as they watch Her Voudoun children drown.

Clifton Cay

We are bodies of water.
Bodies in water like islands
We are thirsty
For the rawness of seawater.
We are hungry

For a Bathing Pool Baptism.
Pinch of coral rock on bare soles,
We are chained ankle to ankle,
Unable to dance
Like Sea Oats swaying

In a salty breeze.
We have been seaweed
Scrubbed and de-liced
Ready for Vendue House.
Yet our watery bodies

Relive a mating chant,
Our spirits swirl like waterspouts,
Blood pounds our veins
like Junkanoo drums.
HurricaneLightningOya CommandsUs:

Run naked breasts swinging
through tamarind groves,
Run to the bluegreen sea,
Immerse your cerulean selves,
Remember flesh and bone.

An Ode to Peace

My garden mocks me savagely
Pride of Barbados flowers bloom
Yellow-trimmed-orange-red explodes
Cremation fire heat

Tightly curled cerise rose buds spurt
Out whorls of coagulated
Blood that carpets the earth purple
Muffling banshee screeches

In underground tunneled subways
In mountain caves of darkened night
Mogadishu to Mucurapo
Kabul to Calcutta

In the beams of my car's headlights
Scarlet specks of giant moth's eyes
Sail kamikazi style into
My radiator fins

Dying embers of greybrown ash
What if I had prescienced
This sign perhaps written these words
Perhaps I could have warned

Maybe what if I remembered
Tower of babel voices loud
And a mighty earthquake roaring
Perchance written this poem

Immortelle and Bhandaaraa Poems

Could I have prevented terror
From Palestine to Port-of-Spain
New York City to Nassau Town
Jerusalem the rock

Could I have air-lifted and bombed
The world with a plane-load of peace
Of Hummingbirds and Night Jasmine
Sweet-scented love for all

Could I have mimicked with this ode
My garden full of life and death
In cycles of sunshine and dark
A prayer for Om Shanti

What If The B-S Axis Revolved Around Maha Lakshmi

Yo Mama Lakshmi, Goddess of Peace
Show these guys your colours so bright
Pink for love, yellow for friendship

Yo Mama Lakshmi, Goddess of Peace
Show these guys your wealth and knowledge
Flowing from deya lights not bombs

Yo Mama Lakshmi, Goddess of Peace
Show these guys your lotus lilies
Sacred and serene prized among flowers

Yo Mama Lakshmi, Goddess of Peace
Sound these guys your sitar music
Haunting echo in valleys deep

Yo Mama Lakshmi, Goddess of Peace
Teach these guys to meditate true
Ponder your gifts of wisdom and light

Yo Mama Lakshmi, Goddess of Peace
Flood the world with holy nectar
Honey and milk to drown all wars

Yo Maha Lakshmi, Goddess of Peace
Jaya Hai! Victory to You!

No-People Land

It is just useless so stop de ole talk
Start a new talk, a harder day morning
Forget de serpent, find yourself a wuk
Dream the Great Mother in a cave mourning

While Our Father in heaven reigning
Children ah de earth have hungry bellies
Full up big with gas and malnu paining
De angels fly away from dem smellies

Dey ent touching no blood, snat and tear stains
To dirty up dey white robes and wing tips
Let de Mother and she helpers make gains
Rise up in dem shanty towns tattered slips

Of no-people land behind-God-back place
Not a mountain or seashore Asgard
Not a Paradise so full ah grace
Just a bubbly, muddy Devil's Woodyard

Full with rotten-egg fumes ah pig-pen stink
Buh look good, good, see how amoebae thrive
See zygote cells multiply in a blink
Hatching de guppy roe dat survive

Little mermaid goddesses transparent
For dem who can read de message within
Who can start a new talk to make things right
Bellies full with food and faces grinnin

Pink Wall Blues

Six-tenths of a mile so long
Six feet high to the sky
Six-tenths of a mile too long
Six feet reaching to sky
One man/woman European
Gated community

Adam/Eve in Eden
Savages outside the gate
Adam/Eve in the Garden
Savages outside the gate
Five hundred and twelve years
Two months of slavery

Arawak genocide
Pale skins sipping Carib
Lucayan genocide
Pale skins sipping Carib
Blood like communion wine
Conquer the savages

One hundred and sixty-six
Years emancipated
Much as one hundred sixty-six
Years of emancipation
Indentured to the Massa
Still looking for the Wisemen

From the North or the East
To bring us glad tidings
Either from the North or the East
Welcome planeful of glad tidings
Brings an economy so rich
Full of butlers and housemaids

Finally we're inside
The gated community
Finally with Massa inside
The gated community
Savages singing the blues
Safe within the pink wall

Invasive Species on Buck Island, United States Virgin Island

Buck Island

Lone stingray glides like a submarine
Turks Cap cacti perch on the hillside
Surveying all like spirit Tainos
Eleven Bahama ducklings
Crowd together yellow/black fluff
In a three foot manmade pond hole
Fallen ghost crab struggles to climb
Its vertical sandy wall
While a pair of Frigate birds sail
Overhead their shadows crossing

Catamaran that brought
This invasive species to Buck Island
(Nature Reserve sprouting from the sea)
For a Saturday morning frolic
In the aqua water beige sand
Ringed by brown & white sedimentary rocks
Whose vertically eroded ridges
Dig into soft soles like sea urchin spines
No match for the Box Fish which dislodges
And gorges on sea egg delicacies

Then when the sun is noonday high
The catamaran gathers its invasive species
And sails away under the watchman's
Gaze of Turks Cap cacti

Ghost Crab

I felt declawed
Unable to grasp, pinch
The sandy wall to climb
Out of my manmade trap
To scuttle free across the beach
Play hide and seek with the waves
Dance with my mate
Lay eggs and feed my babies
I felt my transparent body
Drying up, crisping in the heat
Becoming morsels of duckling food

Turks Cap Cacti

Our spirits have witnessed
This invasive species
Bringing boats building paths
Walking all over our island
Seeking animals and plants
So-called invasive species
To cull or uproot
Saving (yeah right) the island
That we have guarded
Protected with balls of our fuzz
Since before Taino-time
We gaze and ponder
How much more time
Before we ourselves are uprooted
Become extinct
Just another species
Gone to spirit
On this Buck Island Nature Reserve

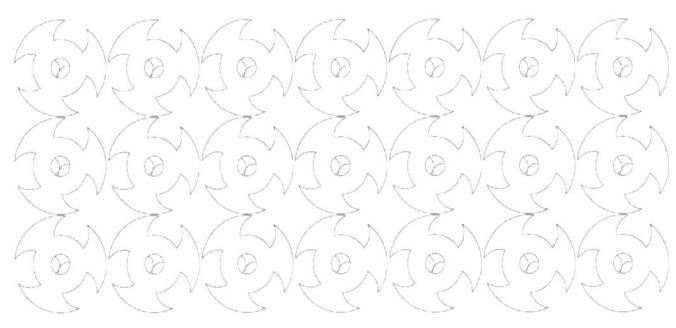

HECATE, QUEEN OF THE NIGHT

WOMEN EVOKED HECATE FOR PROTECTION AND ERECTED HER THREEFOLD IMAGES AT THEIR DOORS

Guardian of the Threshold

Poetry is all about what comes in...
— Robert Kelly

In the half-open light of the gallery
When everyone else is asleep
The hammock creaks rhythmically
Like someone unknown is swinging
In the dark: a jumbie, a tief

The silent enemy wanting
To seep inside through door cracks
Like smoke from the chulha
Waiting to enter the kumbha
Defile and never leave

So seal the door tightly
Keep it from banging flapping
Inviting the intruder
Be the Guardian of the Threshold

Give Me Your Chaff and Grain

I will be a huntress
Artemis-like
Prowling the skies
Orion-like
I will feed you moon-beam *sawine*

I will be your *baldaquin*
Venus-rays-like
Over the Meniscus Moon
At Ramadhan's end
Wish you "Eid Mubarak"

I will cradle you
Mother-Goddess-like
Silver crescent
Sliver moon-child
I will take you to the Celestial

Garden of Delights

Pearl in the Oyster

Green plastic-wrapped
Quarter-inch-thick wire
Strung between Seagrape
Almond, Wild Tamarind trees
Is where I hang my laundry
And think thoughts

Bruised and cut
By taut clothes line
Ochre-green soft bark
Of the Seagrape trunk
Grows outward, copper/plastic
Covered by cortex/phloem

Coated in aseptic green
You believe in breathing space
Blind you cannot see
My scar tissue wrapping
You tightly, you cannot feel
Me sealing you smoothly

Angioplasty you are
My vein ballooner
Pacemaker
Heartsaver
Life Marker
Sand Pearl
In my
Oyster

Vaginal Scan

It is the day after her fifteenth
Wedding Anniversary.
Her vagina is being prodded.

She lies naked from the waist down
on a teak-brown exam table,
watches as deft fingers
spread a bead of ultrasound gel
on the tip of the penis-like probe.

Watches as teeth tear open
the packet, fingers slip the condom
expertly onto the sonic camera
and the tip is re-gelled.

A thumb rests on the testicular-
looking saddle.
The probe swirls her vulva
searching for the opening.
Quickly it is found,

the camera slides into her vagina,
painlessly, smoothly, well-greased.

She breathes slowly
In… Out…
as the cervix is opened. The camera
shoots her womb: perfectly photogenic.

She breathes more calmly
as the camera presses on the sides
capturing flawless follicular cysts,
beauty marks on her ovaries.

My Coontie

The other night I sit down quiet
Minding my own business
Suddenly I hear a shout
"I want to be called by my right name!"
Shit I nearly pole vault outta my skin
"What, who, how you mean?"
"I tired of the name Coontie
From now on I am Vagina
Coontie is a Native American word
meaning flour root
I am no flour root neither no flower
No orchid neither
Just plain Vagina
No saltfish no crabby no bread
Not vinegar Vagina
V-A-G-I-N-A and don't quirt
No vinegar up me neither!
I am no seedbag no gempouch
No money-wallet no sperm deposit box
No squaw that is Native American
For female genitalia not squash
Not pumpkin not coochie or cave
Or slit or clit or penis case
No pussy no cat no pussycat
I am Vagina
And I just want to be called
By my right name!

Bad Hair Night

My hair is bad, it is ownway
It wants to go on the bus
Never mind the knife
Cutlass and gun all the fighting

It wants to experience a bus ride
Through Nassau
On Christmas night
Just before Boxing Day Junkanoo start

It wants to mix up
In OPB (that's other people's business)
Stick up here push out there
I say MYODB (you could guess who business that is)

Keep a low profile
But no my hair bad
My hair wants to be referee
In fight (the ultimate is a Mike Tyson fight)

My hair wants to part
No, like stand up in the middle
Pushing apart
Warring gangs

And make proclamation about sides
Who on the wrong
Who on the right
I say is only one side

I interested in
My own backside
So I outta here
With my bad bad hair

Immortelle and Bhandaaraa Poems

'Two Weeks Later' by Lelawattee Manoo-Rahming

Past Prime Time

Late September Sweet Broom
Blooms golden tan
Fields of fuzzy grains
On stalks thin and bent
At thirty degree angle
In soft breezes

They hurry to ripen
In blazing sun
Before the days shorten
In October
And the season changes
To northwesters

Low pressure arthritic
Joints inflamed red
Yellow orange bonfires
Of Sweet Broom straw
But there are no Stinging
Nettles in place

Of Sweet Broom no patch
To kneel one's knees
No searing pain to make
One forgetful
Of aching stiffness
Of past prime time

Ghazal on Ageing

In my 38th year I discovered old age
Daily bras to cup sweaty sagging breasts told age

Blood flows not for a long week but three short-lived days
Normal periods become stingy in golden age

Implantation favours youthful ova not mine
Maybe ovacomdotcom will sell and hold age

Arterial tubes have high materiality
They save hearts of plaque awarded men in mould age

Fallopian tubes get blocked more and more each menses
In the twilight years these tubes are not sold by age

I can buy with e-commerce lifting Wonder Bras
St. John's Wort for menopause relieves cold/hot age

Stocks share and treasury bonds Asha may bring you wealth
Your genome dear never will enrich in dolt age

Immortelle and Bhandaaraa Poems

'Children of Orion' by Lelawattee Manoo-Rahming

Acne on God's Cheek

As the summer sea like glass does not speak
Of temperamental hurricanes within
So the glossy covers of the books
Of our lives do not reveal turbulence
Eruptions of temper lavalike blood
Swirling moments of madness euphoric
Ghoulish dreams lurking behind closed eyelids

Tormented by the meaning of life's death
Are our lives like acne on God's cheek
Manifestation of adolescence
To be tolerated only until
Aloes or some other godly medicine
Can obliterate the painful pustules
Scars and all shadows of our existence?

Or is God menopausally settled
Into a predictable pattern sine
Waves whispering on tropical beaches
Of summer sea not howling hurricanes?
Will our deaths then be salved by aloes clear
Slimy, jellylike, cooling lubricant
So we slip smiling into bright dayclean?

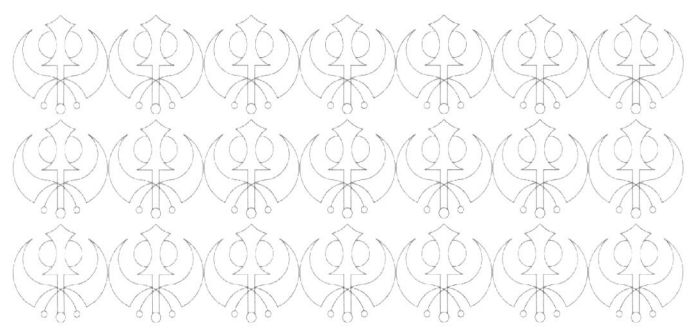

THE GODDESS

AS THE SHAKTI
OR ENERGY OF DIVINITY

SURROUNDS AND ANIMATES

THE ENERGY OF THE MALE GOD

Strong Like Mangrove
For the women of Zonta.

Mama I want to tell you
We have made planks
From your trunk-like legs
Sturdy as Bahama Pines
Dancing in hurricane winds
We have glued these panels
With Pear tree sap scarlet as blood
And made a Thanksgiving table
Wide enough to feed a village
Long enough to see the babies

Mama we have found your recipe
One handful of broken bones
One cupful of tears
Four teaspoons of anger
A pound of *that's-it-no-more*
Two bowls of determination
One packet of survival powder
We have pounded and mixed
Kneaded and baked loaves
To feed the village wide

The babies are growing fat
Creamy as the full moon
Girl children are laughing
Genitals no longer mutilated
Boy children are modelling
Porcelain clay not fondling guns
Men and women are stripping sisal
Making threads knitting families
Strong like mangrove in the salina
We are coming home to you Mama

'Hat with Coconut Rachis' by Lelawattee Manoo-Rahming

Ocean Goddess on a Journey

Allen Ginsberg imagined Walt Whitman
In a California supermarket
But I saw you in a California supermarket
Like one of Gauguin's Tahitian women
Earthy, big-boned, tall
Offering me a white and brown smile.

I wanted to take a long walk with you
Through the lovely streets of San Francisco
Listen to the story of how you journeyed
From your Pacific Island home
In fulfillment of your karma
Your life as a poet.

How you looked for it every morning
As you carefully arranged mangoes
Pineapples, carambolas and pears
Inhaling their sweetness
Beaming yourself back to coconut fields
Reliving batik-wrapped memories.

I wanted you to show me the little
Trellised café you frequented in the evenings
Where the magenta flowers reminded you
Of Frangipani, inspired you to write poems
Allen Ginsbergian and Walt Whitmanish
But tangy with Oceanic goddess energy

Of Great Hina, Creator, Death Mother
Tapa-beating woman
Warrior Queen of the Island of Women
Poems that renewed you in the same way
Goddess Hina was restored
Each time she surfed the ocean's waves.

I wanted to tell you that I too
Come from an island home – in the Caribbean
Where we worship our own Indian and African
Ocean Goddesses – Lakshmi and Yemaya
Offering them hibiscus, coconut, banana
Rejuvenating ourselves in sea baths.

I wanted you to feel the Great Goddess
Lifeforce flowing between us connecting us.
I wished I had let you know
How like a goddess you were
And that I was glad I saw you
In a California supermarket.

Immortelle and Bhandaaraa Poems

The Night the Scorpion Ate the Moon

First half
Then a quarter
Then a crescent
Then a sliver
Until just an ember was left

Glowing dying till the moon
Was just a shadow of its full self
A phantom moon in sandstone red

Planesfullofpeople rumbling beneath
Trains whistling past
But no one saw
The full moon disappearing
Into darkness

No one fell on their knees shrieking
Begging the Sky Mother to save our Moon
From the hungry Scorpion Goddess

We were blinded
By incandescence fluorescence
Neonses nuances of Pink Pussycat
Miami Jai Alai
But the moon must really

Be made of cheese
Sour yellow Camembert maybe
Indigestion causing lactose

For the Scorpion slowly
Regurgitated our Full Moon
First an ember
Then a sliver
A silver crescent

A golden quarter
A yellow half-dollar
A white shiny nickel in the sky

And all was well once again
With planesfulofpeople scooting
Across the moonshine sky
Trains whistling mournfully
In the moonlight

Pink Pussycats still dancing on billboards
And Jai Alai players still batting balls
White as the Full Moon

Written in Miami beneath the eclipsed Full Moon in Scorpio.

The Wild Lover

Cleansing healing saltwater
Bathes my body
Mango juice salty sweet
Drips down my breasts
And I want you

Fleshy coolness yellowmelt
Washed by sea waves
Of yearning for your warmth
Sunshine tingling my bare back

Sunburning with longing
For a cooling spray
Of sea water balm
Or mango butter calming

My tingling nerves
Flushed with desire
For your passion tear

Desert Rose

When a scorching heat dries up
The land the Desert Rose never forgets
To bloom Magenta Powder Pink Red
On fleshy bare stems

She knows when the rains come
Her bell flowers will die
New green leaves will sprout
Greedy for Mother Mokosh's Milk

She spends the rainy season
A spindly-armed comely green
Sister surrounded by Ixora
Buttercup Frangipani debutantes

She grows fatter
But hides her pregnancy
From the Rainbow Goddess Kunapipi
Until her sisters' flowers have withered

She offers a yellow-leaved carpet to Al-Lat
The Desert Goddess who massages her belly
With coal hot hands helping to birth
Drought time queens

Guanahani

If I kissed your seagrape stained lips
Would I taste life acerbic sweet
Salty-tart juices on my tongue?

If I curled my fingers through your hair
Would I feel centuries of living
Rough/smooth edges of coral rock?

If I rested my head on your bosom
Would I hear a primal pulse
Heart beats of a hutia-skin drum?

If I inhaled you reminiscent
Would I recollect infinity
Wet with sea spray suds and spume?

And if I called your name Guanahani
Let it glide like a seagull on the wind
Would you respond, in whale song blues?

Reggae Music

Like salt stars on soucouyant wings
Beres' music glistens in spaces
Interstices between woven threads
Sea Fan veins or spiders' webs
Filling voids with mermen's voices

Maxi's music sparkles in sunlight
Until the next downpour dissolves
Into brine washes out to sea
Silver tones of rhythm
Resonating over hills
Greened by the first storm
The drought ending burst from heaven

Marley's reggae music flashes golden
From the eye's corner
A ball of soucouyant fire
That mirrors the twinkling of stars
In a dark dark night

The Poet
For Lorna Goodison.

A poet is someone
who can pour light into a cup
and then raise it to nourish your beautiful
– perhaps parched – holy mouth
  — Hafiz

A poet is one who finds the rents
The ruptures in our quiltlike cores
Unravels the broken threads
Collects them into balls of fibres
Spins them into rainbow-coloured yarn
Weaves an unpatterned fabric
With which she mends by hand
Gently ever so gently
Crevices in quilted psyches

email to Kamau Brathwaite on his 70th birthday

As an African a plastic bullet hit me in Northern Ireland
But me children overstood and dey grew strong,
As an African I was woman in a man's world,
A man in a computer world,
A fly on de wall of China,
A Rastafarian diplomat,
An a miner in Wales.
I was a red hot Eskimo,
A peace luvin hippie.
   — Benjamin Zephaniah

tolook@me,
I am know African,
doh dey tell me African First Mother Eve's
mitochondria still mark my genes.

tolook@me,
I am knot black diasporan,
I'm brown, so dey say, not a red hot Eskimo.
Oily straight hair? Could be a hippie.

tolook@me,
Is to see Mahatma,
doh my grey-haired temples are more Indira's.
Her portrait adorned my childhood walls.

tolook@me,
Is to c a jhandi,
white/yellow/red flags shredded by northeast trade
winds & rains that flood Chaguanas.

tolook@me,
Is to sea a coolie,
my father was a labourer who cleared drains
@dawn, was pissy drunk @dusk.

tolook@me,
I was born Caribbean,
thirty years in your future to overstand your words;
cut and paste my own.

tolook@menow,
Indo-Trini woman,
poet scouring she way inna Afro-man's world,
wanting@least 70 years, like you.

Immortelle and Bhandaaraa Poems

'Reincarnation' by Lelawattee Manoo-Rahming

The Birthing Season – India in Spring

*My movement dwells in the stillness of my depth,
In the delicious birth of new leaves,
In flood of flowers,
In unseen urge of new life towards the light,*
    — Rabindranath Tagore

Flame of the Forest scorches my vision
Blinds me to the beggar girl with child on hip
Grey eyes piercing my scowling face

Bombax Ceiba flowers scarlet water
Jars of spring quench my thirst for new life
In drought scarred Keoladeo Ghana marshland
Park where the rickshaw cyclist grinned toothlessly
At his first customers in four days

Frangipani blossoms scent my air
With yellow and white perfume masking
Stale B.O. and decaying urine
On New Delhi streets choked with exhaust

Bougainvillea shrubs tall as trees
Fluoresce magenta, crimson, orange
On scoured sandstone Rajasthani hills
Haunting me with an ancient silence
That deafens the elephant's trumpeting

Peepal trees large as giants stand guard
Around Queen Mumtaz's Taj Mahal
Offering me sacred solitude
Away from the vendoring crowds
Waiting patiently to pounce on me
On the outside of the mausoleum

All of these blossomings herald new lives
Movements towards the light
The cycle of spring that births asha
Reincarnation from the depths within
Winter-frozen lifeblood icicles

Finding Shakti

She came from chigger infested
Caroni canefields banking river
Ochre silt to hide alligators
And Mama d'leau water snake
Guabine, coski freshwater fish
Cascadu and swampland blue crab
River conchs and big-mouth tater
Searching for Shakti energy
On the Yamuna banks

In the dead Queen mausoleum
 – And how many died to build this?
In the woman and her beti
With firesticks bundling their heads
Heading home in dusky shadow
Of the bejewelled Taj Mahal
Their only jewels the nose rings
Silver bracelets, bright coloured clothes
On the Yamuna bank

And found Rani Durgawati
Warrior statue on Agra chowk
Bare-breasted Lakshmi tempera
KN Majumdar's red vision
Of the goddess cross-legged
On an eagle not a lotus
Ravi Varna's saintly Sita
Giving herself to Mother Earth
On the Yamuna bank

Immortelle and Bhandaaraa Poems

The Goddess power Shakti
Creatrix of the universe
Life giver to Lord Brahma
Not hidden by a purdah veil
Not burnt as Sati offering
Not silent and subservient
But mounting a lion slaying
Demons, invaders, conquerors
On the Yamuna banks

Divali 2003

Deepavali, New Moon, no moon
Day moon, darkest amavasya
Time falls back into a deya
Fire curling shimmering
Like an agile goddess.

Wisps of coconut-oil-incensed
Smoke crevice the air diffusing
Into lungs, prayerful hearts and minds

Dispelling darkness, ignorance
Poisonous, fleecy, parasitic
Thoughts: meditate on Maha Lakshmi
See time fall back into myriad
Full moon orbs, little deya lights
On the darkest amavasya

And know that the darker the night
The brighter the light: a traveler's
Beacon hanging high in the sky
On a bamboo pole. Goddess
Goodness in a mangod time
"Shub Divali".

Parang Serenade in Two Parts

I

It wasn't your song.
No Rio Manzanares did you beg,
"Dejame pasar," neither
Did you open the door
When paranderos cajoled,
"Abreme la puerta! Abreme la puerta!"

Los esposos Maria y Jose
Van desde Nazareth,
But you climbed
Onto a donkey cart,
Burrowed deeper into tall, tall,
Sugar canes La Paille, Caroni, Morong.

Quatro and mandolin Din Din Din,
Es hora de partir,
Did not rouse you from a coir mattress
Sleep that only Cannes Brulee
Sweet smoke sugarcane fire
Could rouse you awake in Petit Careme.

Las maracas Clap Clap Clap,
Bottle and spoon Ping Ping Ping.
Daisy Voisin Parang Queen,
Sereno sereno her pagnol rhythm
As foreign as ground beef pastelle.
You never ate sacred Mai Gaay

Immortelle and Bhandaaraa Poems

Nor did you speak español.
Your lights weren't candles at Christmas
But deyas at Divali.
El nino Jesus was no Baby Krishna blue
And Jesus' birthday went with rum,
Curry manicou and chutney.

II

But I have songs for you my mothers
In my blood. I take you with me
My Ajee, my Nani, my Mowsee
My Kaakee, my Daadee, my Phoowaa.
I serenade "Dejame pasar Rio Caroni,"
On my way to Chacachacare,

"Dejame pasar Rio Valencia,"
On my way to Toco,
"Dejame pasar Rio Ortoire,"
On my way to Guayaguayare,
"Dejame pasar Rio Guapo,"
On my way to Icacos.

I sprinkle your ashes on every corner
Of this Iere, Land of the Hummingbird.
I absorb parang through my pores.
I partake of pastelle and puncha crema.
I understand, "Din, din, din,
Es hora de partir."

"Din, din, din, camino de Belen,
Los esposos van desde Nazareth."
I know the Christmas story,
The gift of Baby Jesus born in a manger,
And how in his name Guanahani
Became San Salvador,

Then sugar become king.
They crossed you over the Kala Pani,
But when you cried, "Darvaza kholna prasann!"
No one understood you.
All they knew was, "Abreme la puerta!"
And they kept the door closed.

Pero ven, ven aqui mi Ajee, mi Nani,
Mi Mowsee, Kaakee, Daadee, Phoowaa.
Come, walk with me,
I have opened the doors for you,
Vaya con dios, "Shubh Christmas,
Naya saal mubarak ho!"

The Poet

Lelawattee Manoo-Rahming is an engineer, a poet, fiction and creative non-fiction writer and essayist. Her poetry and stories have appeared online and in numerous publications in The Bahamas, the Caribbean, the USA and Europe, including *WomanSpeak*, a Bahamian literary journal featuring women's voices; *The Caribbean Writer*, the University of the US Virgin Islands literary journal; *Anthurium*, a Caribbean Studies electronic journal, published by the University of Miami; *Poui: The Cave Hill Literary Annual*, University of the West Indies, Cave Hill, Barbados; *Voice, Memory, Ashes: Lest We Forget*, an anthology published by Mango Publishing, UK; *In Our Own Words – A Generation Defining Itself*, a literary journal edited by Marlow Peerse Weaver, published by MW Enterprises, NC, USA; *Hampden-Sydney Poetry Review Special Caribbean Issue (2004)*, University of Virginia; *Yinna*, Journal of the Bahamas Association of Cultural Studies (BACUS); *Journal of Caribbean Literatures*, University of Central Arkansas; and *Thamyris*, a literary journal published by Najade Press, Amsterdam.

She was a featured writer at the Miami Book Fair International (1996 and 2000); the Mary Lou Williams Center for Black Culture, Duke University, 2002; and the University of The Virgin Islands, St Croix Campus Humanities Week, 2004. She was the Keynote Speaker at the Caribbean without Borders Conference 2008, at the University of Puerto Rico.

Lelawattee has participated in several writing workshops including the University of Miami Caribbean Writers' Summer Institute Fiction Workshop (1994, on a Fiction Scholarship) with Olive Senior, and Poetry Workshop (1995, on a Poetry Scholarship) with Lorna Goodison; the Cropper Foundation Fiction Workshop (Trinidad, 2000) with novelist Merle Hodge and Short

Fiction writer Funso Aiyejina (on a Cropper Foundation Scholarship); the Women In Literature and Letters (WILL) writing workshops held at New York University (1998), studying with Lorna Goodison in the Poetry Workshop and Donna Masini in the Fiction Workshop; and the OAS/CARICOM "Writing Children's Literature" Workshop (Jamaica, 2000) which she attended on a scholarship.

Lelawattee also expresses her creativity and seeks enlightenment through sculpture, drawing and painting. She has won poetry, essay and art awards in The Bahamas. Internationally, she has won the David Hough Literary Prize from *The Caribbean Writer* (2001), the Canute A. Brodhurst Prize for Short Fiction from *The Caribbean Writer* (2009), and was the Overall Winner of the Commonwealth Broadcasting Association 2001 Short Story Competition. Her first book of poetry, *Curry Flavour*, was published in 2000 by Peepal Tree Press, Leeds, England. Her second poetry collection, Immortelle and Bhandaaraa Poems, was short listed for the inaugural international Proverse Prize (2009) for unpublished writing, administered by Proverse Hong Kong.

Lelawattee, who was born in Trinidad, is married to Bahamian, Hammond Rahming, and makes her home in Nassau, The Bahamas, where she is a practicing Mechanical/Building Services Engineer. Her academic qualifications include a B.Sc. Degree in Mechanical Engineering (Hons) from the University of the West Indies, St. Augustine, Trinidad; and an M.Sc. Degree in Building Services Engineering from Heriot-Watt University, Edinburgh, Scotland. She is a Chartered Engineer registered with the UK Engineering Council.

The Preface Writer

Sandra Pouchet Paquet taught Caribbean literature and culture at the University of Miami from 1992 to 2010, where she directed the Caribbean Writers Summer Institute from 1992-1996 before starting the Caribbean Literary Studies Program in 1999. In 2003, she founded *Anthurium: a Caribbean Studies Journal,* and served as the editor of that journal from 2003 to 2010. Professor Paquet is the author of *The Novels of George Lamming* (1982), *Caribbean Autobiography* (2002), and co-editor of *Music, Memory, Resistance*: *Calypso and the Caribbean Literary Imagination* (2007). She has published widely in Caribbean literature in leading journals in the field. She retired from the University of Miami in 2010 and continues her research and scholarship, as well as editing and teaching.

Paquet's research interests include the areas of Caribbean literary and cultural studies, diaspora studies, and autobiography.

Glossary (including place-names, cultural explanations and notes on persons named) and Notes
~~ Compiled by Lelawattee Manoo-Rahming and Gillian Bickley, both separately and co-operatively.

Note on Poetic Forms used
Poetic Forms used in *Immortelle and Bhandaaraa Poems* include the following:
The Catalogue Poem (used loosely, as Manoo-Rahming notes, in 'Memory Catalogue' and 'Healing After Hurricanes Frances and Ivan');
The rhyming quatrain ('No-People Land' and 'Bhandaaraa Puja for Sundar Popo Uncle');
The Sestina;
The Pantoum;
The Ghazal.

GLOSSARY AND NOTES[5]

3canal: A Rapso music band in Trinidad and Tobago. (Rapso is a hybrid of calypso and rap music.)

Abeer (*Hindi*): A red dye made into a liquid and sprayed onto observers and devotees during Phagwa, a Hindu festival celebrated in Trinidad and Tobago, which is also known as Holi in India. The red liquid leaves an indelible stain when, as a prank, it is mixed with banana sap.

Achall: In Irish legend, Achall was a loving sister who died of sorrow when her brother was killed in battle. Her love was memorialized at the Hill of Achall near Tara, the island's mystic centre. (Source: Patricia Monaghan, *The New Book of Goddesses and Heroines*, Llewellyn Publications, St. Paul, Minnesota, USA, 1997.)

Adam/Eve: Adam and Eve, who according to the Book of Genesis were

---
[5] **Reference**
Many of the Trinidad and Tobago Creole, French Creole, Spanish Creole and Bhojpuri Hindi words were cross-referenced using, *A Dictionary of the English/ Creole of Trinidad and Tobago*, edited by Lise Winer, published by McGill-Queen's University Press, Montreal and Kingston, Canada, 2009.

the first man and woman on earth.

Aedon: The queen of ancient Thebes plotted to murder the eldest son of her rival Niobe but accidentally killed her own child. Stricken by remorse and grief, Aedon attempted suicide and was transformed into the first nightingale, a bird that still haunts the night with its mournful cry. (Source: Patricia Monaghan, *op. cit.*)

Agwe: Haitian sea-goddess. Agwe is another name for the great goddess of Africa and of the African diaspora, Ymoja. Among her numerous names in the African diaspora, Ymoja is called Agwe in Haiti. Ymoja is also syncretized with Our Lady of Regla and Mary, Star of the Sea. (Source: Patricia Monaghan, *op. cit.*)

Airmed: An ancient goddess of Ireland. After her beloved brother Miach died, she buried him with great mourning. Innumerable plants, all the world's herbs, sprang from his grave. As Airmed tended Miach's grave, the herbs instructed her in their use, thus she became the goddess of witchcraft and herb lore. (Source: Patricia Monaghan, *op. cit.*)

Ajaa (*Bhojpuri Hindi*): Paternal grandfather.

Ajee (*Bhojpuri Hindi*): Paternal grandmother.

Al-Lat: 1) Allāt, pre-Islamic Arabian goddess, one of the three chief goddesses of Mecca; 2) al-Lat, ancient name for the Sun in Frank Herbert's *Dune* universe. 3) Al-Lat is a mythic figure of great antiquity, one of the trinity of desert goddesses named in the Koran, Al-Uzza and Menat being the others. (Source: Patricia Monaghan, *op. cit.*)

Aldebaran: An orange giant star located about sixty-five light years away in the zodiac constellation of Taurus.

Aloe: a plant genus containing many species, some of which are used for medicinal and beauty purposes. The gel in the leaves of Aloe vera, for example, can be made into a smooth type of cream that can heal burns such as sunburn. (*Wikipedia*)

Althaea (Mother Althaea): This Greek woman had two sons. One of them, Meleager, was a hero in campaigns against tribal enemies and the other (unnamed) was a priest of secret rites. When Meleager killed his brother, the priest, their mother, Althaea, cried out to the underworld to take the murderer away. (Source: Patricia Monaghan, *op. cit.*)

Amavasya (*Hindi*): The 15th day of the dark fortnight, that is the fortnight of the waning moon, coinciding with the date of the new moon.

Amchar Massala (*Bhojpuri Hindi*): A mixture of spices ground into a powder, used for making pickles of unripe fruit.

Androsia batik: Androsia is a batik fabric and batik clothing manufacturing factory located on the island of Andros in The Bahamas. The fabric is locally called Androsia batik.

Arawak: The Arawak People are some of the indigenous inhabitants of the Caribbean. The Indigenous peoples are collectively called Amerindians.

Arena Dam: The name of a dam in Trinidad and Tobago, a major source of potable water.

Artee (*Hindi*): A Hindu ritual, performed during a puja, in which a small fire in a deya (see "diya lights" below) is moved in a circular motion in front of the image of a deity to receive a blessing.

Artemis: Greek goddess of wisdom, a huntress, daughter of Zeus.

Asgard: 1) Legendary capital of King Arthur's Camelot.
2) In Norse mythology, Asgard was one of the nine worlds, and home of the Gods, which was connected to heaven by a rainbow bridge. (*Wikipedia*)

Asha (*Hindi*): A female proper name meaning "hope".

B-S Axis: The Bush-Saddam Axis, a neologism created by Manoo-Rahming.

Baisakh: The second month of the Hindu calendar, roughly corresponding to April in the Gregorian calendar.

Balata (scientific name: *Manilkara bidentata*): commonly called Balata in Trinidad and Tobago. This is a large evergreen tree whose fruits are reddish-brown berries about an inch in diameter. (Source: *Native Trees of Trinidad and Tobago* by Victor C. Quesnel and T. Francis Farrell, with photography by Paul L. Comeau, published by The Trinidad and Tobago Field Naturalists' Club, Port of Spain, Trinidad and Tobago,

2000). The fruit, which has a sweet, juicy, slightly gummy, edible pulp, is also called Balata.

Baldaquin: silk brocade with silver and gold threads.

Baljugnee (*Bhojpuri Hindi*): Firefly.

Banshee: This spirit woman is said to appear to Irish families to foretell the coming death of one of its members. She can choose not to be seen, instead conveying her message of bereavement by producing an unearthly keening sound outside the window. (Source: Patricia Monaghan, *op. cit.*)

Baralgin: A pain-relieving medication, usually prescribed for pain with spasms.

Battimamselles (*Trinidad and Tobago French Creole*): dragonflies.

Bay Street: The main street in Nassau, the capital of The Bahamas.

Ben Lion kaiso riddum: "Ben Lion" is the name of a song by 3canal and Andre Tanker. Kaiso is another word for "calypso". "Riddum" (*Trinidad and Tobago English Creole*) means "rhythm".

Beti (*Bhojpuri Hindi*): Daughter or girl.

Bhagwan (*Bhojpuri Hindi*): God.

Bhakti (*Bhojpuri Hindi*): Religious devotion.

Bhandaaraa (*Bhojpuri Hindi*): Religious ceremony held twelve or thirteen days after a death.

Bhavani (Goddess Bhavani): a ferocious aspect of the Hindu goddess Parvati. Bhavani means "giver of life", the power of nature or the source of creative energy. In addition to her ferocious aspect, she is also known as "Karunaswaroopini" ("filled with mercy").
    Bhavani was the tutelary deity of the Maratha leader Shivaji, to whom she presented a sword. A temple to Bhavani at Tuljapur in Maharashtra dates back to the 12th century. The temple contains a meter-high granite icon of the goddess, with eight arms holding weapons. She also holds the head of the demon Mahishasura, whom she slew in the region which is the present day Mysore. (*Wikipedia*)

Immortelle and Bhandaaraa Poems

Bhojpuri Hindi: The dominant Indian language in Trinidad and Tobago, closely related to Hindi, which was brought to Trinidad and Tobago by Indian indentured servants.

Big Bang Jouvert Jab Jab: A term created by Manoo-Rahming using the following terms: "Big Bang" is a reference to Andre Tanker's song "Children of the Big Bang". "Jouvert" (*Trinidad and Tobago French Creole*) is the pre-dawn opening parade on carnival Monday morning. "Jab Jab" (*Trinidad and Tobago French Creole*) is a traditional carnival devil character, usually played during Jouvert.

Blackface: The name of one of Manoo-Rahming's beloved cats.

Blanchisseuse: The name of a village and beach in Trinidad and Tobago.

Blockarama / Blockorama (*Trinidad and Tobago English Creole*): A large, loud, outdoor party, usually held in a street that has been closed off to vehicles.

Bois Cano (literally, "wood for canoe") (*Trinidad and Tobago French Creole*): a medicinal plant known for its healing, cooling and soothing properties.

Bombax Ceiba: Scientific name for the Red Silk Cotton tree which is common in India.

Boundary ball for six (cricketing term): If the batsman hits the ball a certain distance and it reaches a particular part of the pitch in any direction, he scores six runs.

Box fish: The local Bahamian name for the cowfish, which is a member of the trunkfish family.

Brahma (Lord Brahma): the Hindu god (deva) of creation and one of the Trimurti, the others being Vishnu and Shiva. According to the Brahma Purana, he is the father of Mānu, and from Mānu all human beings are descended. In the Ramayana and the Mahābhārata, he is often referred to as the progenitor or great grandsire of all human beings. He is not to be confused with the Supreme Cosmic Spirit in Hindu Vedānta philosophy known as Brahman, which is genderless. Brahmā's consort is Sāvitri and Gāyatri. Saraswati sits beside him, the goddess of learning. Brahmā is often identified with Prajapati, a Vedic deity. (*Wikipedia*)

Brathwaite, (Edward) Kamau (1930-): born in Bridgetown, Barbados. His poetry traces historical links and events that have contributed to the development of the black population in the Caribbean and is distinguished by its experimental linguistic (and often multilingual) explorations of African identity in the West Indies. He is also the author of two plays and several collections of essays and literary criticism. (*Wikipedia*)

Brazzalita wood: A Bahamian variation of the name "Braziletto", which is botanically allied to *Caesalpinia echinata*, the Scientific name for Brazil Wood. The wood is reddish in colour and is traditionally used for carvings.

Buan: This Irish heroine had the psychic power of understanding her husband after his death. When his severed head was brought home to her, she asked it questions about how he was killed, translating the faint reddening and whitening of the flesh to gain her answer. Understanding that he had died by treachery, she cried herself to death. The magical hazel tree Coll Buana grew from her grave as a testimony to her steadfast love. (Source: Patricia Monaghan, *op. cit.*)

Buck Island, US Virgin Islands (Nature Reserve): Buck Island is a small, uninhabited, 176 acre island about 1.5 miles north of the northeast coast of St. Croix, United States Virgin Islands. It was first established as a protected area by the U.S. Government in 1948. Along the trail are plaques with information about marine flora and fauna commonly found in the area. (*Wikipedia*)

Bougainvillea: stunningly coloured flowering vine, named after Admiral Louis de Bougainvillea, who "discovered" it in 1768.

Buljol roast bake lavway: A term created by Manoo-Rahming using the words, "Buljol", "Roast bake" and "Lavway", explained as follows:
- "Buljol" (*Trinidad and Tobago French Creole*) is a dish in Trinidad and Tobago made with flaked, rehydrated, salted codfish, sliced tomatoes, onions and hot peppers mixed in hot oil.
- "Roast bake" is a dish in Trinidad and Tobago. It is a circular, thick but flattish bread, made with water, flour and baking soda.

- "Lavway" (*Trinidad and Tobago French Creole*) is a traditional word for song or melody in Trinidad and Tobago.

Caimate: A Trinidadian variation of the name "caimito" (scientific name: *Chrysophyllum cainito*). The rounded, green- or purple- skinned fruit is edible, with sweet, whitish pulp.

Carailli (*Bhojpuri Hindi*): The Trinidadian variation of the Hindi word "karela", which, in English, is more commonly known as bitter melon or bitter gourd. The leaves of the plant are brewed and drunk as herbal medicine for colds and flu.

Carambola: The fruit of the tree *Averrhoa carambola*, it is also known as star-fruit because of the five-pointed shape of the cross-section. When ripe, the fruit is edible with a sweet and juicy pulp.

Carib: The name of a beer produced in Trinidad and Tobago. Carib is also the name of one of the Amerindian group of peoples inhabiting the Lesser Antilles, after whom the Caribbean Sea was named.

Carman: In Irish legend, she was goddess of malevolent magic who could destroy anything by chanting her spells. Her three sons – Dub (darkness), Dother (evil) and Dian (violence) – wreaked havoc with their bare hands. (Source: Patricia Monaghan, *op. cit.*)

Caroni: A river in Trinidad and Tobago.

Caroni: Caroni County takes its name from the Caroni River. It stretches from the hills of the Central Range into the lowlands of the Caroni Plains and the Caroni Swamp. It is heavily associated with sugar cane and the Sugar Belt, but actually accounts for no more than one third of the sugar belt. The now-defunct state-owned sugar company, Caroni (1975) Ltd took its name from the county. Caroni County occupies 557 km² (215 square miles) in the west central part of the island of Trinidad, the larger island in the Republic of Trinidad and Tobago. It lies south and southwest of Saint George County, west of Nariva County and north of Victoria County. To the west it is bounded by the Gulf of Paria. County Caroni includes the town of Chaguanas, the largest town (by population) in the country. Administratively it is divided between the Borough of Chaguanas, the Couva-Tabaquite-Talparo Regional Corporation and the Tunapuna-Piarco Regional Corporation. The county was divided into four Wards: Chaguanas, Couva, Cunupia and Montserrat. (*Wikipedia*)

Immortelle and Bhandaaraa Poems

Cascadu: Alternative spelling of "cascadura", a flat-headed, edible, armoured, freshwater fish of Trinidad and Tobago.

Catalogue: Manoo-Rahming notes: "I have used the Catalogue Poem loosely ('Memory Catalogue' and 'Healing After Hurricanes Frances and Ivan')."

Caura: a river in Trinidad and Tobago.

Chacachacare: Now an abandoned island in the Republic of Trinidad and Tobago. The island was spotted by Christopher Columbus on his third New World voyage on 12th August 1498, and his little fleet spent the night anchored in Monkey Harbour. He named the island "Port of Cats" because many wildcats lived on the island.

At various times in its history Chacachacare has served as a cotton plantation, a whaling station, a barracks for US Marines and a leper colony. (*Wikipedia*)

Chador: Alternative spelling of the Hindi word "chadar", which is a bed sheet used to cover oneself, that is, the flat sheet in a set of bed sheets.

Chaguanas: The name of a town in Trinidad and Tobago.

Chamelli: Alternative spelling of the Hindi word "chameli", which is the Crape Jasmine [*sic*], the flowers of which are used in Hindu worship.

Champa (*Hindi*): Frangipani flowers, used in Hindu worship.

Châtaigne (seeds) (*French*): also known as breadnuts. (The breadnut tree is related to the breadfruit tree and the jackfruit tree.) The young breadnut fruit is curried and served as a vegetable. The seeds of the ripe fruit are boiled in salted water, shelled and eaten as a snack. They taste like roasted chestnut. Hence the name, "châtaigne", which in French means, "chestnut".

Chigger: The larval stage of burrowing mites that can infest humans and other animals.

Chimmies: Plural of "chimmy", the Bahamian name for the warbler bird, a year-round resident in The Bahamas.

Immortelle and Bhandaaraa Poems

Chinitat (*Bhojpuri Hindi*): This was the name given to Trinidad during the period of Indo-Caribbean Indenture (1838-1920). It means, "Land of sugar and sweetness" and it was used by the recruiters to entice the Indian labourers to journey to Trinidad.

Chowk (*Hindi-Urdu*): a place where paths intersect. (*Wikipedia*)

Chulha (*Bhojpuri Hindi*): Earthen stove.

Chutney spirit: A neologism created by Manoo-Rahming. "Chutney" (*Bhojpuri Hindi*) is a type of Indian song with a fast rhythmic beat. "Chutney spirit" refers to the trancelike quality of the beat.

Chutney Soca Crown: This term refers to the crowning of the winner of the Chutney Soca Monarch competition, one of the many carnival competitions held in Trinidad and Tobago during the annual carnival season.

Clifton Cay: A village in The Bahamas which has been designated as a Heritage Site because it contains ruins of one of the earliest slave settlements in The Bahamas.

Coatrischie: Tempest-raising goddess of the Antilles.

Coll Buana: See "Buan" above.

Coral Bean tree: Scientific name: *Erythrina pallida*, a medium-size tree native to Venezuela and the West Indies. The seeds are scarlet with a black spot.

Cortex (from Latin: "bark", "rind", 'shell' or "husk"): in Anatomy, the outermost or superficial layer of an organ.

Coski (*Trinidad and Tobago Creole*): A shortened version of the word,"coscorob", which is an edible freshwater fish with iridescent blue markings.

Cosmic tree: A religious and mythological motif, in which a colossal tree (with its branches in the heavens) connects the heavens, the earth and (through its roots) the underworld.

Crease (cricketing term): name of the position where a batsman stands to receive the ball from the bowler of the other side.

Crepe Coq (*Trinidad and Tobago French Creole*): A soft-stemmed native shrub (scientific name: *Centropogon cornutus*), which grows along moist shady banks and in cocoa fields. The flowers are bright magenta in colour.

Crestle greens (*Trinidad and Tobago English Creole*): Watercress.

Crooked Island Passage: A much-frequented sea channel on the leeward side of Acklins Island and Crooked Island in The Bahamas.

Cyar (*Trinidad and Tobago English Creole*): Can't.

Demeter: Greek goddess and mother of Persephone. When Persephone disappeared into the underworld, the weeping Demeter searched and searched but could not find her. As Demeter mourned, all the plants wilted and shriveled. After a while, when Persephone was returned to her mother, spring bloomed again on the earth. (Source: Patricia Monaghan, *op. cit.*)

Detroit Pistons: One of the teams in the American National Basketball Association (NBA), based in the state of Michigan.

Devi (*Sanskrit*): Goddess.

Deya / deya lights (also "diya", "divaa", "deepam", or "deepak"): The name Divali (see below) is a contraction of the word "Deepavali", which translates into "row of lamps" (in Sanskrit). Divali involves the lighting of small clay lamps (diyas) filled with oil to signify the triumph of good over evil.

Dharu (moonshine dharu) (*Bhojpuri Hindi*): Home-made rum.

Dholak (*Hindi*): A large, cylindrical, Indian drum, played with the hands on both ends.

Dilly: The Bahamian name for the Sapodilla fruit (scientific name: *Manilkara zapota*).

Dingolay (*Trinidad and Tobago French Creole*): Dance with fancy, elaborate movements.

Dinsley Plain: A poetic phrase created by Manoo-Rahming using the following words: "Dinsley", which is the name of a village in Trinidad and Tobago, and "Plain" which refers to the location of the village in the flat land at the base of the Northern Range of mountains.

Divali: (also spelt Diwali) or Deepavali: popularly known as the festival of lights; an important five-day festival in Hinduism, Sikhism and Jainism, occurring between mid-October and mid-November. It is an official holiday in Trinidad & Tobago. (Adapted from *Wikipedia*.)

Drupatie / Young Drupatie: Drupatie Ramgoonai is a chutney and chutney-soca artiste in Trinidad and Tobago. The phrase "Young Drupatie" was created by Manoo-Rahming to indicate that Drupatie is a young artiste who followed in the footsteps of Sundar Popo.

Dub, Dother, Dian: See "Carman" above.

Duck egg: "out for a duck" is a cricketing term for scoring nil.

Durga (Goddess Durga): In Hinduism, Durga (Sanskrit, "the inaccessible"; Bengali, "the invincible") or Maa Durga (Bengali, "Mother Durga") – "one who can redeem in situations of utmost distress" – is a form of Devi, the supremely radiant goddess, depicted as having ten arms, riding a lion or a tiger, carrying weapons and a lotus flower, maintaining a meditative smile, and practicing mudras, or symbolic hand gestures.
 An embodiment of creative feminine force (Shakti), Durga exists in a state of svātantrya (independence from the universe and anything/anybody else, i.e., self-sufficiency) and fierce compassion. Kali is considered by Hindus to be an aspect of Durga. Durga is also the mother of Ganesha and Kartikeya. She is thus considered the fiercer, demon-fighting form of Shiva's wife, goddess Parvati. Durga manifests fearlessness and patience, and never loses her sense of humour, even during spiritual battles of epic proportion. (Adapted from *Wikipedia*.)

Durgawati (Rani Durgawati): the daughter of Raja Salivahan of Rath, a king of the Chandela dynasty. She marked her name in the history of India by combining beauty and grace with courage and wisdom. She married Dalpat Shah, the ruler of the Gondwana Empire in central India. After the death of her husband, she took up control of the province on behalf of her minor son, Bir Bahadur, and ruled from 1548 to 1564. She was a good administrator, great warrior, and liberal patron of learning. The empire flourished during her reign. She extended her frontier and accomplished the political unification of Gondwana.

Durgawati won great success against Baz Bahadur, the Sultan of Malwa. In 1564, the Mughal Emperor Akbar attacked the empire. A vigorous battle was fought between the Queen and the aggressors. Durgavathi was seriously wounded and her son was killed. She lost the war and committed suicide by plunging her dagger into herself to escape from dishonour.
(Text slightly adapted from "Rani Durgawati / Dani Durgavati", Online Highways LLC, http://www.india9.com/i9show/Rani-Durgawati-43544.htm, 7 June 2005.)

Eden, Garden of: the original home of the first man and woman, Adam and Eve, according to the Book of Genesis. Also known as, "Paradise".

"Eid Mubarak": traditional Muslim greeting, at the end of Ramadan, meaning "Happy Eid".

Filmi gita: A phrase created by Manoo-Rahming from the following words: In India, "filmi" refers to the music and songs from popular Indian movies. "Gita" (*Hindi*) means "song". Indian movies are popular in Trinidad and Tobago and the music and songs are regularly performed by musicians of Indian ancestry.

Five Fingers tea: Tea made from the leaves of a medium-sized tree (scientific name: *Tabebuia bahamensis*). The leaves are palmately compound with five oval leaflets, hence the local Bahamian name, "Five Fingers". The tea is consumed as a refreshing beverage and as herbal medicine.

Flame of the Forest: tropical tree with stunning red flowers.

Frigate birds: Seabirds, sometimes called Man of War birds or Pirate birds.

Ganga Mai (*Hindi*): Mother Ganga, goddess after whom the river Ganges was named.

Garden in Lebanon: An oblique reference to the Song of Solomon in the King James Version of the Christian Bible, chapter four, verse fifteen, "A fountain of gardens, a well of living waters, and streams from Lebanon".

Gauguin, Paul: French artist (1848-1903), known for his paintings of Polynesian people and scenes, and buried in the Marquesas Islands,

Immortelle and Bhandaaraa Poems

French Polynesia.

Gaulin crab: A medium-sized land crab found in The Bahamas which is eaten by the Night Heron. The local Bahamian name for the Night Heron is "Gaulin", hence the crabs are called "Gaulin crabs". The shell of the crab is blackish red which bleaches to pink after the crab dies.

Genome: "In modern molecular biology and genetics, the genome is the entirety of an organism's hereditary information. It is encoded either in DNA or, for many types of virus, in RNA. The genome includes both the genes and the non-coding sequences of the DNA." (*Wikipedia*)

Gesso: A white paint mixture of glue, chalk or gypsum, and pigment used to prepare the surface of canvas prior to painting.

Ghazal: An Ancient Persian form of verse. It is a collection of two-line poems, and these two-lined poems are called "shers".
   In a ghazal, the second line of each sher must end with the same word(s) and this feature is called "radif". Each word before each radif must rhyme with each other and this rhyme is called, "kaafiya".
(See, "What is a Ghazal?" an article that Abhay Avachat posted on < rec.music.indian.misc>.
See also: <http://smriti.com/urdu/ghazal.def.html>.)
   In *Immortelle and Bhandaaraa Poems*, the poem, "Ghazal on Aging", obeys these rules.

Ghee (*Hindi*): Clarified butter.

Ghungrus (*Hindi*): Bells worn around the ankles in traditional Indian dance.

Ginsberg, Allen: American poet (1926-1997).

Goat Pepper (*Bahamian English Creole*): Hot pepper (scientific name: *Capsicum chinense*), used in cooking.

Gobar (*Bhojpuri Hindi*): A cow dung and water mixture used to plaster floors.

Goodison, Lorna: Jamaican poet (1947-), a leading West Indian writer of the generation born after World War II.

Googlie (cricketing term): special type of delivery of the ball by the bowler to the batsman, very difficult both to deliver and to play.

Grandbeti: A neologism, meaning "granddaughter", created by Manoo-Rahming using the words: "grand" (*English*) and "beti" (*Bhojpuri Hindi*) which means daughter.

Great Goddess: This term comes from the theory that each ancient religion had a Great Goddess as the primary deity, sometimes referred to as the Great Mother.

Great Mother: See "Great Goddess" above.

Grouper Days: A neologism created by Manoo-Rahming referring to good fishing days. The grouper is a commercial food fish, common in The Bahamas.

Guabine: belongs to the family Erythrinidae, a group of ichthyophagous fishes that can be dangerous if handled carelessly. When they bite, their jaws lock on their prey. (J.S. Kenny, *The biological diversity of Trinidad and Tobago: A Naturalist's notes*, Prospect Press, Port of Spain, Trinidad and Tobago, 2008, p. 22.) Freshwater fish of Trinidad and Tobago.

Guanahani: the name the natives gave to the island that Columbus called San Salvador when he arrived at the Americas. Columbus reached the island on 12 October 1492, the first island he sighted and visited in the Americas. Guanahani is one of the islands of the Lucayan archipelago in The Bahamas, but the exact island is a matter of some debate. (*Wikipedia*)

Guppy: A small fresh or brackish water fish found in Trinidad and Tobago. It can be found in clear mountain streams, in polluted canals, or in drainage ditches.

Hammond, Beres (born Hugh Beresford Hammond, 28 August 1955, Annotto Bay, Saint Mary, Jamaica): a reggae singer known in particular for his romantic lovers' rock and soulful voice. (*Wikipedia*)

Hanuman: Monkey God in the *Ramayana*.

Hari Krishna (*Sanskrit*): A mantra recited to invoke spiritual consciousness in Lord Krishna worship.

Hari Rama (*Sanskrit*): A mantra recited to invoke spiritual consciousness in Lord Rama worship.

Hecate (also "Hekate"): a Greco-Roman goddess associated with the underworld, magic and crossroads. She has been associated with childbirth, nurturing the young, gates and walls, doorways, lunar lore, torches, dogs, witchcraft, curses. (Adapted from *Wikipedia*.)

Hina (1): The Polynesian Great Goddess, Hina is a complex figure associated with many aspects of life and symbolised in many ways. She is the tapa-beating woman who lives in the moon; she is Great Hina, the death mother; and she is a warrior queen of the Island of Women. On the Island of Women, Hina is an ageless and beautiful leader. Whenever she begins to show her age, she goes surfing and comes back renewed and restored. (Source: Patricia Monaghan, *op. cit.*)

Hina (2): (literally "girl") is the name of several different goddesses and women in Polynesian mythology. In some traditions, the trickster and culture hero Maui has a wife named Hina, as do the gods Tane and Tangaroa. Hina is often associated with the moon and with death. (*Wikipedia*) See "Hina" above.

Holy word lessons: lessons based on a religious text.

Hurucan (*Amerindian*): The name of an Amerindian god, possibly of Carib origin, who was the god of thunder, lightning and wind, from which the present-day word, "hurricane", is derived.

Hutia: a rodent, the only indigenous land mammal in The Bahamas.

Immortelle: Scientific name: *Erythrina poeppigiana*. A tall tree with vermillion flowers. The trees used to be planted as shade trees in the cocoa plantations of Trinidad and Tobago.

Indira: Indira Ghandi, Indian politician, daughter of Jawaharlal Nehru.

Isis: This ancient Egyptian goddess lived with her beloved brother, Osiris, god of Nile waters and the vegetation that springs up when the river floods. Osiris was killed by their evil brother, Set. The mourning Isis cut off her hair and tore her robes to shreds, wailing in grief. Eventually Isis was able to retrieve her beloved's body. Inventing the rites of embalming, she applied them with magical words to the body of Osiris, bringing him back to life. (Source: Patricia Monaghan, *op. cit.*)

Ixora: a tropical plant.

"Jaya Hai!" (*Hindi*): literally translated as "Victory is".

Jerry-curled: A neologism created by Manoo-Rahming based on the jerry curl hairstyle in which the hair is loosely curled.

Jhalla (*Hindi*): A high energy rhythm in Indian music.

Jook (*Caribbean Creole*): stab, pierce, prick. In Trinidad and Tobago, "jook" also means to scrub clothes using a washing board. The Trinidad and Tobago word for washing board is "jooking board".

Jumbies / jumbie bird (*Trinidad and Tobago Creole*): "Jumbie" means ghost. "Jumbie bird" is a local name for the owl, whose sombre call at night was believed to signal an imminent death.

Junkanoo (*Bahamian Creole*): The annual Christmas-time festival in The Bahamas, which has survived from the days of slavery. The festival consists of groups of costumed revelers who dance to the rhythmic beat of goatskin drums, cowbells and brass horns.

Junkanoo Dance: See "Junkanoo" above.

Kaiso (*Trinidad and Tobago Creole*): Calypso.

Kal Yug (*Hindi*): The last of the four stages that the world goes through according to Hindu scriptures.

Kala Pani (*Hindi*): Literally translated into "black water". It refers to the deep, dark ocean that the Indian indentured servants had to cross on their journey from India to the West Indies.

Karma (*Hindi*): The religious concept of the cycle of cause and effect.

Katha (*Hindi*): A group of people gathered to listen to the recitation of Hindu scripture.

Keoladeo Ghana: The Keoladeo National Park or **Keoladeo Ghana** National Park – formerly known as the Bharatpur Bird Sanctuary –in Rajasthan, India is a famous avifauna sanctuary. (*Wikipedia*)

King of Kosala: A reference to the mythic kingdom of Kosala, mentioned in the Ramayana, and to Lord Rama as its king.

Krishna (literally "the dark one"): A deity worshipped across many traditions in Hinduism in a variety of perspectives. While many Vaishnava groups recognize Krishna as an avatar of Vishnu, other traditions within Krishnaism consider him to be svayam bhagavan, or the Supreme Being.
Krishna is often depicted as an infant or young boy playing a flute as in the Bhagavata Purana, or as a youthful prince giving direction and guidance as in the Bhagavad Gita. The stories of Krishna appear across a broad spectrum of Hindu philosophical and theological traditions. They portray him in various perspectives: a god-child, a prankster, a model lover, a divine hero and the Supreme Being. The principal scriptures discussing Krishna's story are the Mahabharata, the Harivamsa, the Bhagavata Purana and the Vishnu Purana.

Kumbha (*Hindi*): Literally translates into pot, jar or pitcher, and is symbolic of the womb.

Kunapipi: In Australian aboriginal mythology, a great mother goddess and the patron deity of many heroes. She is eternally pregnant and is sometimes represented as a rainbow snake. She gave birth to human beings as well as to most animals and plants. She is also the overseer of initiations and puberty rituals. (Source: Patricia Monaghan, *op. cit.*)

LA Lakers: Los Angeles Lakers, one of the teams in the American National Basketball Association (NBA), based in the state of California.

Lakshmi (Hindu goddess of Peace): Lakshmi is the Hindu goddess of wealth, prosperity (both material and spiritual), light, wisdom, fortune, fertility, generosity and courage; and the embodiment of beauty, grace and charm. Representations of Lakshmi are also found in Jain monuments. Mahalakshmi brings good luck to her devotees. She is believed to protect her devotees from all kinds of misery and money-related sorrows.
Lakshmi in Sanskrit is derived from its elemental form lakS, meaning "to perceive or observe". This is synonymous with lakṣya, meaning "aim" or "objective". The Hindu Sacred Texts Vedas call Mahalakshmi, Lakshyayidhi Lakshmihi, which means she is the one who has the object and aim of uplifting mankind.
Goddess Mahalakshmi is called Shri or Thirumagal, because she is endowed with six auspicious and divine qualities or Gunas, and also

because she is the source of strength even to Lord Narayana. She is the consort of Vishnu and married Rama (in her incarnation as Sita) and Krishna as Radha and later Rukmini). (*Wikipedia*)
In some Indian myths, Goddess Lakshmi sprang up from the ocean when it was churned by the gods. Thus she is also revered as a sea goddess. Lakshmi is one of the goddesses worshipped by Hindus in the Caribbean.

Lakshmi Maha / Lakshmi Mata: Maha (Hindi) means Great and Mata (Bhojpuri Hindi) means Mother. Thus Maha Lakshmi means Great Goddess Lakshmi and Lakshmi Mata means Mother Lakshmi.

Lakshmi tempera: Water colour and tempera painting, called "Goddess Lakshmi", by the artist K.N. Majumdar.

Lanka: Sri Lanka.

Lara: The famous cricketer Brian Lara, a national of Trinidad and Tobago.

Lbw: Leg before wicket (cricketing term): one of the ways of the batsman becoming "out".

Legba: A West African god who has survived among the African Diaspora. He opens and closes the doorway to the spirit world.

Loa: In West African mythology, which has survived among the African Diaspora, the "loa" are the spirits who act as intermediaries between the creator deity and humanity.

Long Wharf: An area for docking boats in Nassau, The Bahamas.

Lucayans / Lucayan genocide: the Lucayans were the native peoples of the Lucayan Islands. Within a generation of the arrival of the Spanish, they were extinct.
Interesting information about the Lucayans can be found at: <http://www.flmnh.ufl.edu/caribarch/nativesoftci.htm>.
"They populated islands like Saint Lucia and Martinique until Carib Indians chased them north, to the much less hospitable Bahamas."
(Erik Gauger, in "Notes from the Road", as quoted in, WB, "Lucayans: a culture forever lost", *The World Culture Journal*, 26 August 2002, <http://www.webdak.com/garchives/00000063.html> edited and

published by WebdaK Communications.)

Macaripe: The name of a beach in Trinidad and Tobago.

Machel: Machel Montano, a famous soca artiste in Trinidad and Tobago.

Maha Devi (*Hindi*): Great Goddess

Maha Lakshmi (also Lakshmi Maha / Lakshmi Mata): See previous entry under Lakshmi Maha/ Lakshmi Mata.

Mahatma: Mahatma Gandhi, Indian politician and statesman.

Mahisa (*Hindi*): In Hindu mythology, Mahisa was an evil god who was defeated in battle by Goddess Durga.

Malhar (*Hindi*): A melody in classical Indian music, believed to be so powerful, that when it is sung, it brings torrential rainfall.

Malju (*Trinidad and Tobago Spanish Creole*): From the Spanish "mal de ojo", which literally translates into "bad eye" or "evil eye".

KN Majumdar: A portrait of "Lakshmi" by K.N. Majumdar (1891-1975) is in the Fine Art Gallery, New Delhi, India (ref. FAG 011). She is sitting on an eagle, but there are lotuses in the picture too.

Malnu: A neologism created by Manoo-Rahming, short for "malnutrition" and/or those suffering from malnutrition.

Mama D'Leau (also known as the Mother of the River): protector and healer of all river animals. According to the folklore of Trinidad and Tobago, she usually appears as a beautiful woman with long, golden hair who sits on a rock at the river's edge. When angered, Mama D'Leau becomes serpent-like with each strand of her hair turning into a living snake. An armour of shining scales covers her upper body and arms, and from her waist downwards twists into coils. Her tongue becomes forked and she holds a golden comb which she passes through her snaky hair. (*Wikipedia*)

Mamoo (*Hindi*): Maternal uncle.

Mango butter: has beneficial moisturizing properties for lotions and acts as a mild lubricant for the skin. (*Wikipedia*)

Manicou: Opossum.

Manioc (*Amerindian*): Cassava.

Manzanilla beach: A beach in Trinidad and Tobago.

Mapepire (*Trinidad and Tobago Creole*): A venomous snake found in Trinidad and Tobago.

Marley: Robert Nesta "Bob" Marley, OM (6 February 1945 – 11 May 1981) was a Jamaican singer-songwriter and musician. He was the rhythm guitarist and lead singer for the ska, rocksteady and reggae bands The Wailers (1964–1974) and Bob Marley & The Wailers (1974–1981). Marley remains the most widely known and revered performer of reggae music, and is credited with helping spread both Jamaican music and the Rastafari movement to a worldwide audience. (*Wikipedia*)

Mass Transported: A neologism created by Manoo-Rahming, based on the name of a piece of artwork by the Bahamian visual artist John Beadle, "Mass Transportation", which portrays the plight of illegal migrants who arrived in The Bahamas by boat from Haiti.

Matura: a river in Trinidad and Tobago.

Maxi Priest: British reggae musician.

Meleager: See "Althaea (Mother Althaea)" above.

Meniscus moon: Crescent moon.

Miach: See "Airmed" above.

Miami Jai Alai: a bat and ball game and also a gaming (gambling) club in Miami, Florida.

Middle Passage: The triangular area of the Atlantic Slave Trade, in which ships, laden with goods, set out from European ports, arrived in African ports where Africans were purchased or kidnapped, and then went on to the Caribbean, where the Africans were sold into slavery. The ships then returned to Europe and the cycle began again.

Mike Tyson; American boxer and heavyweight champion. Throughout his career, Tyson became well-known for his ferocious and intimidating boxing style as well as his controversial behavior both inside and outside the ring. (*Wikipedia*)

Miramen mai: Mother Miramen. Miramen is a proper name derived from the Hindi proper name "Mira", which means saintly woman.
Mitochondria: the cell's power producers. They convert energy into forms that are usable by the cell. (*Wikipedia*)

Mogadishu: Capital of Somalia.

Mokosh: a Slavic goddess of water, fertility, and weaving. Rain was perceived as Mother Mokosh's milk, so she was invoked in time of drought. (Source: Patricia Monaghan, *op. cit.*)

Monks, Joe (1901-1994): Bahamian visual artist.

Moonlight glory flower: Also known as Moon Vine (scientific name: *Ipomoea macrantha*). A night-blooming relative of the morning glory. The sweet-scented flowers are white and tubular.

Mother Agwe: See "Agwe" above.

Mount Kailash: Holy mountain in the Himalyas. Abode of Lord Shiva.

Mount Mandara: In Hindu mythology, believed to be the abode of Lord Krishna.

Mucurapo: A town in Trinidad and Tobago.

Mumtaz (Queen Mumtaz Mahal): wife of Muslim Emperor Shah Jahan (died 1666 C.E.), who built the Taj Mahal in her memory at Agra, India. (<www.cyberistan.org/islamic/tajmahal.html >)

Nada Brahma (*Hindi*): Literally translates into the sound of God.

Nana (*Hindi*): Maternal grandfather.

Nani (*Hindi*): Maternal grandmother.

Nassau: The capital of The Bahamas.

Neonses: A neologism created by Manoo-Rahming based on the idea of neon lights.

Never Dirty: a river in Trinidad.

Nino (*Spanish*): Baby boy.

Northwesters: winds from the North West.

Obeah (*Caribbean Creole*): A folk system of magic, based primarily on West African rituals.

Om shanti (*Hindi*): A religious chant which loosely translates into "oh peace".

Orion: character in Greek and Roman mythology; a giant and a great hunter, son of Neptune / Poseidon and Euryale the Queen of the Amazons; given the gift of wading through the depths of the sea (or, some say, of walking on the surface of the sea) by his father. He was killed in error by the goddess Artemis / Diana, with whom he was a favourite. (Another version says he was killed by a scorpion.) A clear presentation of the two myths is given by Cathy Bell in <http://comfychair.org/~cmbell/myth/orion.html>, which was originally prepared for the Princeton University course CLA 212.

Oval: a famous cricket pitch and cricket club in London where visiting cricket teams usually play. Oval is also a reference to the Queen's Park Oval, a test-match cricket pitch in Trinidad and Tobago.

Oya: A Yoruba goddess of storms and lightning, her name means "she tore" in the Yoruba language. A warrior goddess, she was brought to the New World by the African Diaspora. (Source: Patricia Monaghan, *op. cit.*)

Pantoun / Pantoum: Manoo-Rahming notes: "When I first learnt about the Pantoum, it was said that it was derived from the Malaysian Pantoun so I wanted to use that form of the name."

The pantoum is a form of poetry similar to a villanelle in that there are repeating lines throughout the poem. It is composed of a series of quatrains; the second and fourth lines of each stanza are repeated as the first and third lines of the next. This pattern continues for any number of stanzas, except for the final stanza, which differs in the repeating pattern. The first and third lines of the last stanza are the second and fourth of the penultimate; the first line of the poem is the last line of the final stanza, and the third line of the first stanza is the second of the final. Ideally, the meaning of lines shifts when they are repeated although the words remain exactly the same: this can be done by shifting punctuation, punning, or simply recontextualizing.

The pantoum is derived from the pantun – a Malay verse form – specifically from the *pantun berkait*, a series of interwoven quatrains. An English translation of such a *pantun berkait* appeared in William Marsden's *A Dictionary and Grammar of the Malayan Language* in 1812. Victor Hugo published an unrhymed French version by Ernest Fouinet of this poem in the notes to *Les Orientales* (1829) and subsequent French poets began to make their own attempts at composing original "pantoums". Leconte de Lisle published five pantoums in his *Poèmes tragiques* (1884). Baudelaire's famous poem 'Harmonie du soir' is usually cited as an example of the form, but it is irregular. The stanzas rhyme abba rather than the expected abab, and the last line, which is supposed to be the same as the first, is original.

American poets such as John Ashbery, Marilyn Hacker, Donald Justice, Carolyn Kizer, and David Trinidad have done work in this form. Neil Peart used the form for the lyrics of 'The Larger Bowl (A Pantoum)' on Rush's 2007 album, *Snakes & Arrows* (with one difference from the format listed above).

There is also the imperfect pantoum, in which the final stanza differs from the form stated above, and the second and fourth lines may be different from any preceding lines. (*Wikepedia*)

In *Immortelle and Bhandaaraa Poems*, 'A Pantoun in Pink and White' follows the structure described above with one modification. Line three of the final stanza changes one word in the final line of the previous stanza, thus opening up the meaning of the poem.

Paradise Hill: A small hill in a residential area, called Paradise, in the town of Tacarigua, in Trinidad and Tobago.

Parang: "The term Parang is derived from the Spanish word 'parranda', which means a spree or a fête. Initially it meant a group of four or more men who went to give a parranda at an event – a christening or a birthday celebration. The group sang to the accompaniment of musical instruments. However, in Trinidad, parang came to mean the songs that were sung especially during the Christmas season. What was brought from Venezuela to Trinidad was parranda navideña, which means Christmas parang.

"There are two theories about the origins of Trinidad parang. The first is that the custom was brought to the island by the Spanish colonists who ruled Trinidad from 1498-1797. It continued to flourish after the British took over the island, because of constant interaction between the people of Trinidad and those of Venezuela (The Spanish Main).

"The second theory suggests that the custom came from Venezuela during the Spanish occupation. The cocoa panyols came from Oriente, East Venezuela to work on the cocoa plantations in Trinidad and brought with them this aspect of their culture. Whatever its origins, parang is now an integral part of the cultural landscape of Trinidad and Tobago.

"Parang has become synonymous with merrymaking at Christmas time. Groups of musicians called <u>parranderos</u> go from house to house entertaining members of the community. These visits involve singing and dancing as well as the sharing of food and drink. Today, this type of social paranging only takes place in a few areas in Trinidad.

"The main towns for parang are Arima, St. Ann's, Santa Cruz, St. Joseph, Caura, Mausica, Lopinot, San Raphael and Rio Claro (12). One must of course add Paramin to this list.

"The official parang season runs from October to January 6th (The Day of the Kings or Dia de los Reyes). During this period, various parang groups take part in competitions organized by the National Parang Association of Trinidad and Tobago (NPATT) culminating in Lewah (Les Rois), the feast of the Kings." (http://library2.nalis.gov.tt/Default.aspx?tabid=137)

Paranderos: See "Parang" above.

Peepal tree (*Ficus religiosa*): considered highly sacred in the Hindu religion. People worship the pipal /peepul plant due to its religious significance. (<www.thecolorsofindia.com/peepal/index.html>)

People believe that Lord Vishnu and many other Gods used to reside underneath it. The peepul plant is regarded as the representation of various Hindu Gods and Goddesses. The tree is also believed to be associated with the Mother Goddess during the period of the Indus Valley civilization. People revere the Pipal tree and also perform a puja in its dedication.
(See <http://www.thecolorsofindia.com/peepal/index.html>)

The Sacred Fig (*Ficus religiosa*) or Bo-Tree (from the Sinhala *bo*) is a species of banyan fig native to Bangladesh, India, Nepal, Pakistan, Sri Lanka, southwest China and Indochina. This plant is considered sacred by the followers of Hinduism, Jainism and Buddhism, and hence the name "sacred Fig" was given to it. Siddhartha Gautama is said to have been sitting underneath a Bo-Tree when he was enlightened

(Bodhi), or "awakened" (Buddha). Thus, the Bo-Tree is a well-known symbol for happiness, prosperity, longevity and good luck. Today in India, Hindu sadhus still meditate below this tree, and in Theravada Buddhist Southeast Asia, the tree's massive trunk is often the site of Buddhist and animist shrines. The Hindus do pradakshina (circumambulation) around the sacred fig tree as a mark of worship. Usually seven pradakshinas are done around the tree in the morning time chanting, "Vriksha Rajaya Namah", meaning, salutation to the king of trees. (<http://en.wikipedia.org/wiki/Sacred_fig>)

Phagwa (*Bhojpuri Hindi*): In Trinidad and Tobago, the Hindu spring festival celebrating the end of the old year and the beginning of the new. The name, "Phagwa", is derived from the Hindi "phagun", the month of spring in the Hindu calendar. Phagwa is the same as the Holi (great spring) festival in India. See "Abeer" above.

Phloem: a type of plant tissue, used to transport dissolved substances, sap, around the plant.

Pink Pussycat: a gentleman's club; also a sex objects/toys boutique.

Piparo: A district in Trinidad and Tobago.

Piparo Forest: The forest in the district of Piparo in Trinidad and Tobago.

Pitch Lake: The pitch lake in La Brea, Trinidad and Tobago, is a naturally occurring lake of tar.

Plaque: contributes to clogged arteries.

Poetic forms: Various sets of "rules" followed by poems of certain types. The rules may describe such aspects as the rhythm or metre of the poem, its rhyme scheme, or its use of alliteration. Specific poetic forms have been developed by many cultures. In more developed, closed or "received" poetic forms, the rhyming scheme, metre and other elements of a poem are based on sets of rules, ranging from the relatively loose rules that govern the construction of an elegy to the highly formalized structure of the ghazal or villanelle. (*Wikipedia*)

Poinciana: The local Bahamian name for the Royal Poinciana (scientific name: *Delonix regia*).

Immortelle and Bhandaaraa Poems

Port-of-Spain: The capital of Trinidad and Tobago.

Porterweed (scientific name: *Stachytarpheta jamaicensis*): this plant grows as a weed in Trinidad and Tobago. It is also used as herbal medicine.

Preemie (*Trinidad and Tobago English Creole*): Premature.

Puja (*Bhojpuri Hindi*): A personal, familial, or public Hindu prayer service or worship.

Puja bhajans (*Bhojpuri Hindi*): Bhajans are Hindi hymns sung at pujas (*q.v.*).

Purdah (literally, "curtain"): the practice of preventing women from being seen by men. It takes two forms: physical segregation of the sexes, and the requirement for women to cover their bodies and conceal their form. Purdah exists in various forms in the Islamic world and among Hindu women in parts of India. (Adapted from *Wikipedia.*)

Quirt: A neologism, meaning "squirt", created by Manoo-Rahming from the English word "squirt".

Rachis: In botany, it is the main axis which bears the flowers of the plant.

Rainorama: one of Lord Kitchener's calypsos.

Raj Garden: A reference to the British Raj (British Empire in India). In Trinidad and Tobago, it would refer to the gardens grown by the British colonials, and in which many local people would be employed as gardeners.

Rajasthani hills: located outside Jaipur, India.

Rama (*Hindi*): Lord Rama, one of the deities of Hinduism, whose story is told in the Ramayana.

Ramadhan: ninth month of the Islamic calendar, a month of fasting.

Ramayan / Ramayana are used interchangeably in 'Deya for Ajee' (Manoo-Rahming notes that, in this poem, "The last 'a' in 'Ramayana' is silent.")

Rawan: Alternative spelling of the Sanskrit name, "Ravana". Rawan/Ravana is the primary antagonist in the Ramayana. He is the King of Lanka, who abducts Sita, Rama's wife, precipitating the battle in the Ramayana.

Rikki Jai: Born Samraj Jaimungal, Rikki Jai is a chutney (*q.v.*) and chutney-soca artiste in Trinidad and Tobago.

Royal Poinciana: See "Poinciana" above.

Ruellia: An ornamental plant with purplish flowers. Although not related to the petunia, it is sometimes called Mexican petunia.

Rum Ranee: A neologism created by Manoo-Rahming using the following words: the English word "rum", which is the alcoholic drink; and Ranee (*Hindi*), which means queen.

Salina: The local Bahamian name for an expansive, shallow coastal wetland, typically with mangrove ecosystems.

Sandilands: A village in The Bahamas, which contains the mental asylum. The mental asylum is also colloquially referred to as "Sandilands".

Sando: The shortened name for the city of San Fernando, one of the major cities of Trinidad and Tobago.

Sangeet (*Sanskrit*): Song and music.

Sans humanité (*French*): without humanity or mercy.

Santimanitay (*Trinidad and Tobago French Creole*): From the French term, "sans humanité", (see previous entry), meaning, "without mercy".

Sapat (*Trinidad and Tobago Spanish Creole*): A sandal with a wooden sole and rubber strap across the front of the foot, derived from the Spanish word, "zapato", meaning, "shoe". Sapats are normally handmade by the wearer.

Saraswati / Goddess Saraswati / Saraswati Mai: Saraswati is the goddess of learning and sits beside Brahma. (See "Brahma" above.)

Satanic Verses by Salman Rushdie: *The Satanic Verses* is the fourth novel by Salman Rushdie, published in 1988. Manoo-Rahming first read the book, however, during the passage of Hurricane Floyd through The Bahamas in 1999. The days were dark and the nights even darker as there was no electricity. The mood of the days mirrored the surrealism and dream sequences depicted in the novel and it seemed as if life had become, for a day or two, magical reality created by the wind, rain and darkness during the hurricane.

Sati (also called suttee): a religious funeral practice among some Hindu communities in which a recently widowed Hindu woman either voluntarily or by use of force and coercion immolates herself on her husband's funeral pyre. The practice has been outlawed in India since 1829 and is now rare.
 The term is derived from the original name of the goddess Sati, also known as Dakshayani, who self-immolated because she was unable to bear her father Daksha's humiliation of her (living) husband Shiva. (Adapted from *Wikipedia*.)

Saxons: The name of one of the junkanoo groups in The Bahamas.

Sawine: A Trinidadian food eaten during the Eid celebrations, consisting of lightly parched vermicelli, boiled in a sugar, milk and water mixture, served with raisins and nuts.

Sayamanda: The name of one of the songs by Andre Tanker.

Scorpion Mother: See "Scorpion Goddess", below.

Scorpion Goddess: In astrology, the eighth sign of the zodiac, Scorpio, is associated with feminine energy, represented by the Scorpion Goddess. This Goddess is also called the Scorpion Mother.

Sea Fan: Sea Fans are similar to soft corals, however, they anchor themselves in mud or sand instead of attaching themselves to hard substrates. (*Wikipedia*)

Sea grapes: Fruits of the Sea grape tree (scientific name: *Coccoloba uvifera*), which are borne on grape-like clusters, and which turn red to purple in colour as they ripen, one by one, hence the name Sea grapes. These fruits are edible and can be made into jelly.

Sea grape almond: Two tropical fruit trees found in The Bahamas and the Caribbean. For "sea grape", see "sea grapes" above. Almond is also locally known as "Indian almond" (scientific name: *Terminala catappa*), the fruit of which, when ripe, has an edible nut which tastes similar to the more widely-known Mediterranean almond, *Prunus dulcis*.

Sea oats: A tall, coarse grass (scientific name: *Uniola paniculata*), which grows on seashores in The Bahamas and the Caribbean.

Seventh heaven: In certain religious mythology, it is the highest of the heavens.

Sestina (also, sextina, sestine, or sextain): is a highly structured poem consisting of six six-line stanzas followed by a tercet (called its *envoy* or *tornada*), for a total of thirty-nine lines. The same set of six words ends the lines of each of the six-line stanzas, but in a different order each time; if we number the first stanza's lines 123456, then the words ending the second stanza's lines appear in the order 615243, then 364125, then 532614, then 451362, and finally 246531. This organization is referred to as *retrogradatio cruciata* ("retrograde cross"). These six words then appear in the tercet as well, with the tercet's first line usually containing 6 and 2, its second 1 and 4, and its third 5 and 3 (but other versions exist, described below).

The sestina was invented in the late 12th century by the Provençal troubadour Arnaut Daniel. Elements of it were quickly imitated by other troubadours, such as Guilhem Peire Cazals de Caortz.

The oldest British example of the form is a pair of sestinas (frequently referred to as a double sestina), 'Ye Goat-Herd Gods', written by Philip Sidney. Writers such as Dante, Petrarca, A. C. Swinburne, Rudyard Kipling, Ezra Pound, W. H. Auden, John Ashbery, Joan Brossa, Miller Williams, Elizabeth Bishop, Paul Muldoon and Joe Haldeman are all noted for having written sestinas of some fame. (*Wikipedia*)

Manoo-Rahming's 'Oleander Sestina', follows the description given above, with some variation. It does consist of six six-line stanzas followed by a tercet. The same set of six words does end the lines of each of the six-line stanzas, and they are in a different order each time. The order is the same as that described above. The six words do appear in the tercet as well, but in a different sequence to that described above: the first line contains 1 and 2; the second line, 3 and 4; and the third line, 5 and 6. The other variation is that one of the six ending words appears in variations of itself: "fence in", "fenced-in", "Fencing", "fencing", "fenced-in", fenced-in" and "fencing". This calls attention to this word in particular and suggests that Manoo-Rahming is playing with the idea of being fenced-in by the rules of the sestina form.

Shakti: from Sanskrit *shak* – "to be able", meaning sacred *force* or *empowerment*, is the *primordial cosmic energy* and represents the dynamic forces that are thought to move through the entire universe in Hinduism. Shakti is the concept, or personification, of divine feminine creative power, sometimes referred to as "The Great Divine Mother" in Hinduism. On the earthly plane, Shakti most actively manifests through female embodiment and fertility, though it is also present in males in its potential, unmanifest form.

Not only is the Shakti responsible for creation, it is also the agent of all change. Shakti is cosmic existence as well as liberation, its most significant form being the Kundalini Shakti, a mysterious psychospiritual force. Shakti exists in a state of svātantrya, dependence on no-one, being interdependent with the entire universe.

In Shaktism, Shakti is worshiped as the Supreme Being. However, in other Hindu traditions of Shaivism and Vaishnavism, Shakti embodies the active feminine energy Prakriti of Purusha, who is Vishnu in Vaishnavism or Shiva in Shaivism. Vishnu's female counterpart is called Lakshmi, with Parvati being the female half of Shiva. (*Wikipedia*)

Shaman / shamanic: The terms "shaman" and "shamanic", are derived from the word "shamanism" which encompasses the belief that shamans, practitioners of shamanism, are intermediaries or messengers between the human world and the spirit worlds. Shamans may visit other worlds/dimensions to bring guidance to misguided souls and to ameliorate illnesses of the human soul caused by foreign elements. The shaman operates primarily within the spiritual world, which in turn affects the human world. The restoration of balance results in the elimination of the ailment. (*Wikipedia*)

"Shubh Divali!" (*Hindi*): "Happy Divali!"

Sine Waves: A sine wave is a mathematical function that describes a smooth, repeating oscillation.

Sisal (scientific name: *Agave sisalana*): a plant that yields a stiff fibre traditionally used in making twine, rope and also dartboards. The term may refer either to the plant or the fibre, depending on the context.

Sita: (Sanskrit: meaning "furrow") is one of the principal figures of the

Ramayana, the famous Hindu scripture of epic proportions, which details not only the heroic exploits of Sita's husband Lord Rama, but also the sublime love story between Sita and her husband. As the devoted wife of the seventh avatar of Vishnu, Sita is regarded as the most esteemed exemplar of womanly elegance and wifely virtue in Hinduism. She is also considered to be an avatar of Lakshmi, Vishnu's consort, who chose to reincarnate herself on Earth to provide humankind with a paradigmatic example of good virtue.
("New World Encyclopedia",
<http://www.newworldencyclopedia.org/entry/Sita>)

"Saintly Sita giving herself to Mother Earth on the Yamuna bank" ('Finding Shakti', *Immortelle and Bhandaaraa Poems*): refers to a painting by Raja Ravi Varna, "Sita taken by Goddess Earth".

Sitar (*Hindi*): A plucked, stringed, Indian musical instrument.

Sky Mother: In several world mythologies, there are goddesses who are sky dwelling deities. Sometimes they are referred to as Sky Mother. (Source: Patricia Monaghan, *op. cit.*)

Slam dunk: A slam dunk (or simply a dunk) is a type of basketball shot that is performed when a player jumps in the air and manually powers the ball downward through the basket with one or both hands over the rim. This is considered a normal field goal attempt; if successful it is worth two points. The term "slam dunk" was coined by Los Angeles Lakers announcer Chick Hearn. Prior to that, it was known as a dunk shot. The slam dunk is one of the highest percentage shots one can attempt in basketball as well as one of the most crowd-pleasing plays. (*Wikipedia*)

Soapberry: A tropical hardwood tree (scientific name: *Sapindus saponaria*). The sap has been used for soap; and the fruits, when rubbed between the hands, produce a light cleansing lather.

Soca: type of music started by calypso musician, Lord Shorty, who joined East Indian music and musical instruments with African rhythms. (Roots of Rhythm: Extensions, "Chapter 3, p. 40, <http://www.playdrums.com/pdf/roots/5-RORE_Guide-ch3-steeldrum.pdf>)

Soca chokha: A neolgoism created by Manoo-Rahming using the words, "Soca" and "Chokha". "Chokha" (*Bhojpuri Hindi*) is a puree of mashed roasted vegetable (usually eggplant or tomato), seasoned with onions, garlic, salt, pepper and hot oil, eaten as a vegetable side dish. For "soca", see the "soca" entry above.

Socah: When Lord Shorty joined the East Indian music and musical instruments with African rhythms, he called the resulting music, "socah" (sometimes also written as "sokah" or "sohka"). The term has since been shortened to "soca", see entries above.

Sonny Mann: A chutney (q.v.) artiste in Trinidad and Tobago.

Soucouyant (*Trinidad and Tobago Creole*): An old woman who, at night, sheds her skin, travels as a ball of fire and sucks people's blood, leaving a blue mark.

Sparrow: The common name for the Mighty Sparrow, born Slinger Francisco, a Trinidad and Tobago calypso artiste, also known as The Calypso King of the World. He is also affectionately called, "Birdie".

Spica: The brightest star in the constellation Virgo, appearing in the area of the constellation called "the Virgin's hip".

Spin-ball (cricketing term): some bowlers are "spinners". A spin-ball is difficult for the batsman to play.

Suruj (*Sanskrit*, "Suraj"): alternative spelling for "Suraj", sun god in Hinduism.

Surya: Chief solar deity in Hinduism.

Sweet Broom: A tall grass, typically about three feet high, with fluffy, cream-coloured inflorescence. Brooms can be made from the dried grasses by bundling and tying them together.

Tainos / Taino-time: The Tainos were the pre-Columbian inhabitants of The Bahamas, and the more northern islands of the Caribbean. Taino-time is a neologism created by Manoo-Rahming to refer to the pre-Columbian era when Tainos inhabited these islands. See "Lucayans" above.

Taj Mahal: Built by Muslim Emperor Shah Jahan (died 1666 C.E.), in memory of his wife, Queen Mumtaz Mahal, at Agra, India. (<www.cyberistan.org/islamic/tajmahal.html >)

Tamarind: (scientific name: *Tamarindus indica*); a large, fruit-bearing tree, the fruits of which are also called "Tamarind".

Tanhai (*Urdu*): Loneliness.

Tanty (*Trinidad and Tobago French Creole*): Auntie.

Tapa: bark cloth made in the islands of the Pacific Ocean. (*Wikipedia*) See previous entry, Hina.

Tapia (*Trinidad and Tobago Creole*): A wall constructed of reeds, clay mud and grass, used in the construction of tapia houses, which are also known as dirt houses or mud houses. This used to be a typical house construction method in Trinidad and Tobago.

Tater (big-mouth tater): A freshwater fish, similar to a catfish, with a wide mouth, found in Trinidad and Tobago.

Thompson, Archdeacon William (1933-2000): senior member of the Anglican Church in The Bahamas, murdered in 2000.

Tief (*Trinidad and Tobago English Creole*): Thief.

Toco: the most northeasterly village on the island of Trinidad at the point where the Caribbean Sea and the Atlantic Ocean meet, the closest point in Trinidad to Tobago. The name Toco was ascribed to the area by its early Amerindian inhabitants.

In the early 18th century, Capuchins from Spain came to Toco to convert the Amerindians to Roman Catholicism. The mission village there was named "Mission Village".

Unlike many other areas in Trinidad and Tobago, the land in Toco was not suitable for extensive sugarcane cultivation. Thus, by 1797, there was only one sugar mill in the entire district. However, the land was quite suitable for cotton production. In 1797, there were as many as 59 cotton mills.

By 1881, the population of Toco had grown due to the popularity of the cocoa and coffee industry and the influx of workers from Tobago. In fact, at one point in time, Toco was mainly populated by people from the island of Tobago.

In 1830, the Catholic Church made Toco a parish and dedicated the newly-built Our Lady of the Assumption Church at Mission Village to it. (Adapted from *Wikipedia*)

Tree of Life: English translation of "Lignum Vitae", the National Tree of The Bahamas. *Lignum vitae* is used in herbal medicine and the nutritious fruits are eaten by sheep.

Trini: Trinidadian.

Tumhri (*Sanskrit*): Inspirational song.

Turks Cap cactus: (scientific name: *Melocactus intortus*), is found in dry islands in The Bahamas and the Caribbean. The shape is that of an upright oval barrel, rarely reaching three feet in height. Mature plants develop a red, wooly, vertical terminal structure called a cephalium, which resembles a fez, the red felt hat worn by Turks and other eastern Mediterranean men, hence the common name, "Turks Cap cactus". (Source: David W. Nellis, *Seashore Plants of South Florida and the Caribbean*, Pineapple Press, Inc., Sarasota, Florida, 1994.)

Varna, Ravi (Raja Ravi Varna, 1848-1906): Indian painter from the princely state of Travancore who achieved recognition for his depiction of scenes from the epics of the Mahabharata and Ramayana. His paintings are considered to be among the best examples of the fusion of Indian traditions with the techniques of European academic art.

Varma is most remembered for his paintings of beautiful sari-clad women, who were portrayed as shapely and graceful. His exposure in the west came when he won the first prize in the Vienna Art Exhibition in 1873. He is considered among the greatest painters in the history of Indian art.

Veena (*Sanskrit*): A plucked, stringed Indian musical instrument. In images of the Goddess Saraswati, she is shown playing the veena.

Vendue House: An historical building in Nassau, The Bahamas, which was built some time during the eighteenth century. Slaves, cattle and imported goods were auctioned off at Vendue House during the era of slavery.

Vibuthi (*Sanskrit – vibhuti*): Divine attributes such as magnificence, splendour, glory and prosperity.

Voudoun: An alternative (and less stigmatised) spelling of the word "voodoo", which is a religion in the African Diaspora, consisting of elements of African religions syncretised with elements of Christianity.

Walcott, Derek: A Caribbean poet, playwright, writer and visual artist, was born in St. Lucia, in 1930. He won the Nobel Prize for Literature in 1992. He was the first Caribbean writer to win that prize and the second Caribbean national to win a Nobel Prize, the first being Sir Arthur Lewis, who won the Nobel Prize in Economics, in 1979. Derek Walcott's work has had a major influence on Manoo-Rahming who has a childhood memory of watching Walcott's play, *"Dream on Monkey Mountain"* and being mesmerized by it. (Manoo-Rahming was seven years old when the play was written.) Subsequently, Manoo-Rahming was inspired by Walcott's poetry and admired his ability to work in several literary genres as well as the visual arts. His activism in the fields of theatre and literature is exemplary in the Caribbean.

Whe-whe: Playing whe-whe is a form of gambling based on numbers associated with dreams.

Whirling Dervish: A dervish is the common name for an initiate of the Sufi path. One of the ways in which dervishes remember God is through the practice of whirling, which is really a form of religious dancing. These dancing dervishes are sometimes called "whirling dervishes".

Whitman, Walt: American poet (1819-1892)

Windies: Affectionate name for the West Indies cricket team.

Yajna (*Sanskrit*): Worship and sacrifice, usually through the fire sacrifice in which ghee, grains, spices and aromatic wood are offered into a fire according to Hindu scriptures.

Yamraj (*Sanskrit – Yama Raja*): Lord of Death in Hindu mythology.

Yamuna: (sometimes called Jamuna or Jumna), the largest tributary river of the Ganges (Ganga) in northern India. (*Wikipedia*)

Yemaya: Caribbean African Ocean Goddess. (See "Ymoja" below.)

Ymoja chip: A neologism created by Manoo-Rahming using the words, "Ymoja" and "chip", explained immediately below:
> Ymoja is one of the great goddesses of Africa and the African Diaspora. She is the Yoruba goddess of the Ogun River, where she is said to be the daughter of the sea into whose waters she empties. She is also the mother of waters – Mama Watta – who gave birth to

all the waters of the world. Among the African Diaspora, she remains a popular divinity, whose other names include "Yemanja" in Brazil, or "Yemaya" in Cuba, "Agwe" in Haiti, and "La Balianne" in New Orleans. (Source: Patricia Monaghan, *op. cit.*)

"Chip" (*Trinidad and Tobago English Creole*) refers to a rhythmic movement, consisting of small, shuffling steps, used for moving through the streets to music during Carnival.

Zonta: A worldwide organization of executives in business and the professions, working together to advance the status of women. (*Wikipedia*) ~~~

'PARANG SERENADE IN TWO PARTS': NOTE, GLOSSARY AND REFERENCES

Manoo-Rahming notes: "The poem draws on the history of Trinidad and Tobago, in particular Spanish colonization as well as the importation of African slaves and Asian indentured servants. The poem also speaks to the cultural (including language) divide that existed in colonial days (which still exists on some levels) between the Indo and non-Indo populations of Trinidad and Tobago. In the poem, I am attempting to use my knowledge of the languages to bridge the divide and help create a space for my ancestors, in the multicultural fabric of Trinidad and Tobago."

"Dejame pasar": Part of the chorus of the parang (q.v.), 'Río Manzanare', goes like this:

"Rio Manzanare
Déjame pasar
que mi madre enferma
me mando llamar"

("Manzanare river
Let me pass
Because my mother is ill
And she sent to call me")

The Parang, 'Nosotros Tenemos', contains the words,
"Ábreme la puerta y venga a recibirnos" ("open the door for me and let us in").

The Parang, 'Vamos Vamos Vamos', has the words,

"Vamos Vamos Vamos
Es hora de partir
Adorar al Ninoesta en Belen"

("We are going, we are going, we are going
It's time to leave
To worship the Christ child in Bethlehem")

(<http://library2.nalis.gov.tt/Default.aspx?PageContentID=80&tabid=146>)

In this poem, Manoo-Rahming also quotes the following:

"¡Din, din, din! Es hora de partir.
¡Din, din, din! Camino de Belén.
Los esposos van desde Nazareth."

(Villancico navideño: La Jornada, 9 November 2009, <http://navidad.es/2389/villancico-navideno-la-jornada/#more-2389>)

'PARANG SERENADE IN TWO PARTS': GLOSSARY AND REFERENCES

Abreme la puerta (*Spanish*): open the door for me please.

Ajee (*Hindi*): paternal grandmother.

Camino de Belen (*Spanish*): on the road to Bethlehem.

Cannes Brulees (*French*): In the eighteeth century, the early Canboulays were part of the slaves' end-of-harvest celebrations. After emancipation, the people began to represent this scene as a kind of commemoration of the change in their condition, and the procession of Canne Brulee (Burnt Cane) used to take place on the night of 1 August (Emancipation Day).
     The Canboulay festivities have now merged with Carnival Celebrations.
(Adapted from <http://grenada.strabon-caraibes.org/index.php?option=com_content&view=article&id=97>)

Clap Clap Clap: Onomatopoeic rendering of the sound and rhythm of music played.

Daadee (*Hindi*): father's elder sister.

Daisy Voisin: Alexandra "Daisy" Voisin (1924–1991), parang singer and composer.
   Voisin was born in Erin, Trinidad and Tobago. She began her singing career in the Village Council and other local groups. A deeply religious person, she received the message to spread the gospel of Parang in a church in Siparia in 1973. Not long after she was launched into the spotlight at a "Best Village" competition in 1971. She did her best to live up to that calling.
   Hailed as the undisputed "Queen of Parang" for her vocal prowess and the many triumphs and popularity of the band she led, the *La Divina Pastora Serenaders*, Daisy Voisin left an indelible mark on the local Parang scene in Trinidad and Tobago. Armed with her sweet, powerful voice and a bouquet of flowers in hand, she ruled Parang music for countless years. Her signature songs 'Hurray Hurrah' and 'Alegría, Alegría' becoming Christmas classics, sung with her characteristic musical trill, "aiyee, aiyee".
   Her live performances were described as "explosive, vivacious and tempestuous". Voisin and her group became cultural ambassadors for Trinidad and Tobago taking the music to places in the Caribbean, Isla Margarita, Venezuela and North America.
   In the later days of her life, Voisin's performances were few, hampered by ill-health, but the quality of her voice was still evident." (*Wikipedia*)

Darvaza kholna prasann! (*Hindi*): Open the door for me please!

Dejame pasar (*Spanish*): please let me pass.

Deyas at Divali (*Hindi*): small clay lamps lit during the Hindu Festival of Lights.

Din Din Din: Onomatopoeic rendering of the sound and rhythm of music played.

Es hora de partir (*Spanish*): It is time to leave.

Espanol: Spanish.

Guayaguayare (often simply called Guaya): The southeastern-most village in Trinidad and Tobago and the first part of Trinidad and Tobago to have experienced the beginning of a new colonial era with the entry of Christopher Columbus on 31 July 1498.

Guayaguayare was first inhabited by the Amerindians some of whom had become extinct in this region by the time the French had arrived in the 1780s. They are the people responsible for the name of the area and this name survival is one of their last remaining legacies in the country.

It is primarily a fishing village; but it also plays a major role in the petroleum industry.

Guayaguayare was the first area in Trinidad sighted by Christopher Columbus on July 31, 1498. The area along Guayaguyare Bay, between the Lizard River (originally Rio de Iguanas) and the Pilote River (Rio de Pilotas) was settled by French planters and their slaves in the late eighteenth century following the 1783 Cedula de Población.

Guayaguayare also has a prominent place in the history of the oil industry. It was the site of the first commercially viable wells drilled in Trinidad by Randolph Rust and Lee Lum in May 1902.

(Adapted from, "A Brief History of Guayaguayare", Staff Article, July 08, 2006, Posted: July 14, 2006, © 2002 - 2010 TriniView.com, <http://www.triniview.com/places/140706b.html> and *Wikipedia*.)

Guanahani: See main Glossary.

Icacos: Icacos Point is the southwesternmost point in Trinidad and Tobago. It is at the end of a long peninsula that forms St Patrick County. A channel called the Serpent's Mouth separates Icacos Point from the coast of Venezuela, only 11 kilometres away.

Iere: The Amerindian name of Trinidad and Tobago, meaning, "Land of the Hummingbird".

Kaakee (*Hindi*): Paternal uncle's wife.

Kala Pani (*Hindi*) (also *Kalapani*): The Kala Pani (literally, black water) represents the taboo of the sea in Indian culture: sailing the high waves and leaving the mainland meant confronting "houglis" (monsters).

Fear of crossing the Kala Pani also derives from the notion that it entailed the end of the reincarnation cycle, as the traveller was cut off from the regenerating waters of the Ganges. Such voyages also meant breaking family and social ties. This taboo accounts for the lack of interest in overseas commerce on the part of high-caste Hindus, who therefore left this lucrative field to Muslims, and to Christians and Jews settled in the spice enclaves such as Cochin and Calicut.

When slavery was abolished in Mauritius in 1834, the authorities looked for indentured labour to replace the slaves who had been emancipated. The emissaries sent to India for this purpose were astute in attracting so-called "coolies" to the countries (such as South Africa, Mauritius, Fiji and the Caribbean) requiring cheap labour, often presenting these countries as "promised lands".

But many prospective candidates for the distant colonies expressed their fears of crossing the Kala Pani. So the British often employed a stratagem to dispel the doubts of the indentured: they placed water from the Ganges in large cauldrons on the ships, to ensure the continuity of reincarnation beyond the Kala Pani. The sea voyage was then seen as less fearsome.

Mauritian poet and critic Khal Torabully describes the Kala Pani as a source not only of the dissolution of identity, but also of beauty and reconstruction, leading to what he terms a, "coral imaginary". (*Wikipedia*)

In the West Indies too, when slavery was abolished, indentured labour was imported from Asia, particularly, India, China and Java. The term "Kala Pani" was thus brought to the Caribbean by the Indian indentured labourers and has survived to the present day.

La Paille, Caroni, Morong: names of villages in Trinidad. (See also, "Caroni", in main Glossary.)

Land of the Hummingbird: Trinidad and Tobago is known as "The land of the hummingbird", and a hummingbird can be seen on its coat of arms and one-cent coin as well as its national airline, Caribbean Airlines. (*Wikipedia*)

Las maracas (*Spanish*): hand-held clappers.

Los esposos Maria y Jose/Van desde Nazareth (*Spanish*): the husband and wife, Mary and Joseph, leave Nazareth.

Mai Gaay (*Hindi*): Sacred Cow.
Mandolin: Musical instrument from the lute family.

Mowsee (*Hindi*): Mother's sister.

Nani (*Hindi*): Maternal grandmother.

"Naya saal mubarak!": "Happy New Year!"

Paranderos: See main Glossary.

Parang: See main Glossary.

Pastelle: Spanish-influenced ground-(minced-) beef and cornmeal dish, resembling a British pasty. A Christmas delicacy in Trinidad and Tobago.

Pero ven, ven aqui (*Spanish*): But come, come here.

Petit Careme (*French Creole*): In Trinidad and Tobago, there are two seasons: dry, from January to May; and wet, from June to December, with a secondary dry season or *Petit Carême* occurring in September and October.

Phoowaa (*Hindi*): father's younger sister.

Ping Ping Ping: Onomatopoeic rendering of the sound and rhythm of music played.

Puncha creme: A Christmas drink in Trinidad and Tobago, similar to eggnog.

Quatro: Alternative spelling of the word "cuatro" (*Latin American Spanish*) which is a small, four-stringed guitar. The quatro is one of the instruments used to create parang music. See "Parang" above.

Rio (*Spanish*): River.

Rio Caroni: (See main Glossary)

Rio Guapo: Spanish translation of "Guapo River", a river in Trinidad.

Rio Manzanares: A River in Spain, and the subject of a parang song. See "Parang" in Main Glossary.

Rio Ortoire (Ortoire River): At the southern end of Manzanilla Bay; it empties into the Atlantic Ocean.

Rio Valencia: Spanish translation of "Valencia River", a river in Trinidad.

Immortelle and Bhandaaraa Poems

Sereno sereno (*Trinidad and Tobago Spanish Creole*): A typical refrain in parang songs, sung by Daisy Voisin, as well as other paranderos. See "Parang" and "Paranderos" in Main Glossary.

Shubh Christmas! (*Hindi*): Merry Christmas!

Toco: See main Glossary.

Vaya con Dios! (*Spanish*): Go with God!

WRITE TO US!
We are interested to read your comments on
Immortelle and Bhandaaraa Poems
by Lelawattee Manoo-Rahming
Write to our email address, info@proversepublishing.com,
giving us a few sentences
which you are willing for us to publish,
describing your response to this book.
If your comments are chosen to be included
in our E-Newsletter or website,
we will select another title published by Proverse
and send you a complimentary copy.
When you write to us, please include your name, email address
and correspondence address.
Unless you state otherwise, we will assume that we may cut or
edit your comments for publication.
We will use your initials to attribute your comments.

ABOUT PROVERSE HONG KONG

Proverse Hong Kong is based in Hong Kong with expanding long-term regional and international connections. Proverse has published novels, novellas, fictionalized autobiography, non-fiction (including biography, diaries, history, memoirs, sport, travel narratives), single-author poetry collections, children's, teens / young adult and academic books. Other interests include academic works in the humanities, social sciences, cultural studies, linguistics and education. Some Proverse books have accompanying audio texts. Some are translated into Chinese.

Proverse welcomes authors who have a story to tell, wisdom, perceptions or information to convey, a person they want to memorialize, a neglect they want to remedy, a record they want to correct, a strong interest that they want to share, skills they want to teach, and who consciously seek to make a contribution to society in an informative, interesting and well-written way. Proverse works with texts by non-native-speaker writers of English as well as by native English-speaking writers.

The name, "Proverse", combines the words "prose" and "verse" and is pronounced accordingly.

THE PROVERSE PRIZE

The Proverse Prize, an annual international competition for an unpublished book-length work of fiction, non-fiction, or poetry, was established in January 2008. Unusually for a competition of this nature, it is open to all who are at least eighteen on the date they sign the entry form and without restriction of nationality, residence or citizenship.

The objectives of the Proverse Prize are: to encourage excellence and / or excellence and usefulness in publishable written work in the English Language, which can, in varying degrees, "delight and instruct". Entries are invited from anywhere in the world. Semi-finalists to date include writers born or resident in Andorra, Australia, Canada, Germany, Hong Kong, New Zealand, Nigeria, Singapore, Taiwan, The Bahamas, the PRC, the United Arab Emirates, the United Kingdom, the USA.

Founders: Verner Bickley and Gillian Bickley. To celebrate their

lifelong love of words in all their forms as readers, writers, editors, academics, performers, and publishers.
Honorary Legal Advisor: Mr Raymond T. L. Tse.
Honorary Accountant: Mr Neville Chow.
Honorary Judges: Anonymous.
Honorary Advisors: Bahamian poet Marion Bethel; UK translator, Margaret Clarke; UK linguist & lexicographer David Crystal; Canadian poet and academic, Jonathan Hart; Swedish linguist Björn Jernudd; Hong Kong University Librarian, Peter Sidorko; Singapore poet Edwin Thumboo; Czech novelist & poet Olga Walló.
Honorary UK agent and distributor: Christine Penney
Honorary Administrators: Proverse Hong Kong

Proverse Prize Winners whose books have already been published by Proverse Hong Kong:
Laura Solomon (New Zealand), Rebecca Jane Tomasis (Hong Kong & the United Kingdom); Gillian Jones (United Kingdom); David Diskin (UK and Hong Kong), Peter Gregoire (UK and Hong Kong), Sophronia Liu (Hong Kong and USA); Birgit Linder (Hong Kong, Germany); James McCarthy (Scotland, UK); Celia Claase; Philip Chatting.

Summary Terms and Conditions
(for indication only & subject to revision)

The information below is for guidance only. Please refer to the year-specific Proverse Prize Entry Form & Terms & Conditions, which are uploaded, no later than 14 April each year, onto the Proverse Hong Kong website: <www.proversepublishing.com>.
The free Proverse E-Newsletter includes ongoing information about the Proverse Prize.
To be put on the E-Newsletter mailing-list, please email: info@proversepublishing.com with your request.

The Prize
1) Publication by Proverse Hong Kong, with
2) Cash prize of HKD10,000 (HKD7.80 = approx. US$1.00)
Supplementary publication grants may be made to selected other entrants for publication by Proverse Hong Kong.

Depending on the quality of the work in any year, the prize may be shared by at most two entrants or withheld, as recommended by the judges.

<u>In 2016, the entry fee was</u>: HKD220.00 OR GBP32.00.

Writers are eligible, who are at least eighteen on the date they sign The Proverse Prize entry documents. There is no nationality or residence restriction.

Each submitted work must be an unpublished publishable single-author work of non-fiction, fiction or poetry, the original work of the entrant, and submitted in the English language. School textbooks and plays are ineligible.

Unpublished first translations into English (including those already published in the writer's mother tongue) submitted by the author are welcome. The submitted work will not be judged as a translation but as an original work.

<u>Extent of the Manuscript</u>: within the range of what is usual for the genre of the work submitted. However, it is advisable that novellas be in the range 30,000 to 45,000 words); other fiction (e.g. novels, short-story collections) and non-fiction (e.g. autobiographies, biographies, diaries, letters, memoirs, essay collections, etc.) should be in the range, 75,000 to 100,000 words. Poetry / poetry collections should be in the range, 5,000 to 25,000 words. Other word-counts and mixed-genre submissions are not ruled out.

Writers may choose, if they wish, to obtain the services of an Editor in presenting their work, and should acknowledge this help and the nature and extent of this help in the Entry Form.

The regulations are updated from time to time. Please visit proversepublishing.com for updated entry information.

KEY DATES FOR THE PROVERSE PRIZE IN ANY YEAR

(subject to confirmation and/or change)

Receipt of Entry Fees / Entry Documents	[No later than] 14 April to 31 May of the year of entry
Receipt of entered manuscripts	1 May to 30 June of the year of entry
Announcement of Semi-finalists	July-September of the year of entry
Announcement of Finalists	October-December of the year of entry
Announcement of winner/ max two winners (sharing the cash prize)	December of the year of entry to April of the year that follows the year of entry
Cash Award Made	At the same time as publication of the work(s) adjudged the winner / joint-winners of the Proverse Prize
Publication of winning work(s)	In or after November of the year that follows the year of entry

THE PROVERSE POETRY PRIZE (Single Poems)
Summary Terms and Conditions
(for indication only & subject to revision)

The information below is for guidance only. Please refer to the Proverse Hong Kong website: <www.proversepublishing.com> from time to time for full and updated information.

The free Proverse E-Newsletter will include ongoing information about the Proverse Poetry Prize.

To be put on the E-Newsletter mailing-list, please email: info@proversepublishing.com with your request.

This annual international prize, established in 2016, is open to all who are at least eighteen years old, whatever their residence, nationality or citizenship.

Poets may enter in English their own poem(s) previously unpublished in English, in which they own the copyright.

Poems originally written in English and/or poems originally written in another language are equally eligible.

Poems previously published in a language other than English are eligible, provided the writer retains his or her copyright.

If a person other than the poet has translated the poem(s) into English, this must be acknowledged.

Poems may be (a) on ANY subject or theme CHOSEN BY THE POET, OR (b) on a subject or theme, chosen by the Administrators from year to year.

Any form, style or genre may be used.

Poems should be no more than 30 lines each.

Cash prizes are offered as follows: 1st prize; USD100.00; 2nd prize: USD45.00; 3rd prizes (up to four winners): USD20.00.

If sufficient high-quality poems are submitted, a PROVERSE POETRY PRIZE **ANTHOLOGY** will be published by Proverse Hong Kong in a paperback available for online purchase and/or as an ebook, no later than one year after the closing date for entries. All those whose poems appear in any such anthology will be entitled to purchase copies of that anthology AT A DISCOUNT. Poets' names will be published with their poem(s) unless a poet has explicitly stated at the time of entering their poem(s) that they do not wish their name to appear.

If not enough high-quality poems are submitted for an anthology, winning poems will be published online no later than one year after the closing date for entries.

The prizes (if any) will be awarded at the same time as they are published, whether in an anthology or online.

An entry fee needs to be paid for each poem. An entry fee once paid may not be repaid and you may not withdraw a poem from the competition once you have entered it.

Entry Fee: In 2016, the entry fee was: £8.00 for each poem. (Other currencies available: USD12.00, CAD16.00, EUR12.00, NZD18.00, AUD16.00.)

WINNERS will receive an invitation to attend an event in Hong Kong at which, either, the results will be announced and/or any anthology will be launched; and winners will themselves be responsible for all arrangements and costs of attendance, including but not limited to visas, transport, accommodation and meals. If winners are not able to attend, they may be invited to send a brief message which the organisers will consider for reading out or displaying at the event.

No poet may win more than one prize in any year but it is permissible for more than one poem by a single poet to be included in the Proverse Poetry Prize anthology.~~~

POETRY AND POETRY COLLECTIONS
Published by Proverse Hong Kong

If you have enjoyed *Immortelle and Bhandaaraa Poems* by Lelawattee Manoo-Rahming, you may also enjoy the following poetry and poetry collections published by Proverse Hong Kong (all titles in English unless otherwise stated):

Astra and Sebastian, by L.W. Illsley. 2011.

Chasing light, by Patricia Glinton Meicholas. November 2013.

China suite and other poems, by Gillian Bickley. November 2009.

For the record and other poems of Hong Kong, by Gillian Bickley. 2003.

Frida Kahlo's Cry and Other Poems, by Laura Solomon. 2015.
Home, away, elsewhere, by Vaughan Rapatahana. 2011.

Immortelle and bhandaaraa poems, by Lelawattee Manoo-Rahming. 2011.

Irreverent Poems for Pretentious People, by Henrik Hoeg. 2016.
In vitro, by Laura Solomon. 2nd ed. 2014.

Moving house and other poems from Hong Kong, by Gillian Bickley. 2005.

Of Leaves & Ashes, by Patty Ho. *2016.*

Of symbols misused, by Mary-Jane Newton. March 2011.

Painting the borrowed house: poems, by Kate Rogers. 2008.

Perceptions, by Gillian Bickley. 2012.

Rain on the pacific coast, by Elbert Siu Ping Lee. 2013.

refrain, by Jason S. Polley. 2010.

Shadow play, by James Norcliffe. 2012

Shadows in Deferment, by Birgit Bunzel Linder, 2013.

Shifting Sands, by Deepa Vanjani. 2016.

Sightings: a collection of poetry, with an essay, 'communicating poems', by Gillian Bickley. 2007.

Smoked pearl: poems of Hong Kong and beyond, by Akin Jeje (Akinsola Olufemi Jeje). 2010.

The Layers Between, by Celia Claase (Essays and Poems), 2015.

Unlocking, by Mary-Jane Newton. Scheduled, March 2014.

Wonder, lust & itchy feet, by Sally Dellow. 2011.

POETRY– CHINESE LANGUAGE

For the record and other poems of Hong Kong, by Gillian Bickley. Translated by Simon Chow. 2010.

Moving house and other poems from Hong Kong, translated into Chinese, with additional material, by Gillian Bickley. Edited by Tony Ming-Tak Yip. Translated by Tony Yip & others. 2008.

FIND OUT MORE ABOUT OUR AUTHORS BOOKS AND EVENTS AND THE PROVERSE PRIZE

Visit our website
www.proversepublishing.com
Visit our distributor's website
www.chineseupress.com

Follow us on Twitter
Follow news and conversation: <twitter.com/Proversebooks>
OR
Copy and paste the following to your browser window and follow the instructions: https://twitter.com/#!/ProverseBooks

"Like" us on www.facebook.com/ProversePress

Request our E-Newsletter
Send your request to info@proversepublishing.com.

Availability
Most titles are available in Hong Kong and world-wide from our Hong Kong based Distributor,
The Chinese University Press of Hong Kong,
The Chinese University of Hong Kong, Shatin, NT,
Hong Kong SAR, China. Web: chineseupress.com

All titles are available from Proverse Hong Kong and the Proverse Hong Kong UK-based Distributor.

We have stock-holding retailers in Hong Kong,
Singapore (Select Books),
Canada (Elizabeth Campbell Books),
Principality of Andorra (Llibreria La Puça, La Llibreria).

Orders can be made from bookshops in the UK and elsewhere.

Ebooks
Most of our titles are available also as Ebooks.

www.ingramcontent.com/pod-product-compliance
Lightning Source LLC
Chambersburg PA
CBHW041627220426
43663CB00004B/89